"EVEN WONDER WOMAN HAD TO
USE HER AMAZONIAN BERSERKER
RAGE FROM TIME TO TIME..."

CABAL © PUBLISHING

SANTA BARBARA, CA

*Dear Amy,
I owe you my 'wife'. :)
Starshine*

Wife
on the
Edge

CANDID COLUMNS FROM THE BRINK
by

Starshine Roshell

ALSO BY STARSHINE ROSHELL:

KEEP YOUR SKIRT ON:
KICKY COLUMNS WITH LEGS

ISBN 978-0-9766761-4-0

Published in the United States by Cabal Publishing
www.WifeOnTheEdge.com

ISBN 978-0-9766761-6-4

First edition

Cover illustration by Tim Sale
Photograph by Jacky Sallow
Design and layout by John Roshell
TypeKeys font by Typadelic

Printed in the U.S.A.

Visit Starshine on the web at
www.StarshineRoshell.com

For my grandmothers,
two beautiful, strong, funny women
who show me how to be those things,
and love me when I'm not.

CONTENTS

PARENT, THE VERB

BED, WRATH & BEYOND

Acknowledgments

I DON'T WRITE FICTION. My stories aren't spun from imagination; they're patched together from life experience, from the chuckles and worries I share with friends and with strangers in the mammogram waiting room.

Thanks to everyone who willingly feeds me quotes for my columns — and to those who, um, don't know they're being quoted until they see their words in print.

I'm so proud to be a part of the *Santa Barbara Independent*, whose staff does great work and never tells me to "go away" when I wander through the newsroom distracting them from said great work.

Whopping wads of gratitude must be lobbed at the wise Palmer Gibbs for her error-exposing eyeballs; the immoderately funny Kate Schwab for her brilliance in all things booky; publishing sage Richard Starkings for his generosity and counsel; lovely lenswoman Jacky Sallow; and the gifted Rori Trovato of Rori's Artisanal Creamery, whose ambrosial organic homemade ice cream fuels too many late-night writing sessions.

I don't write many columns about how much I rely on my astonishing family because I'm allergic to sappy, and also it's hard to see my computer screen when I'm crying. So let me do it here: Thanks, Mom, for showing me how to be a successful working mother — and for playing Madden Football with my kids so I don't have to. Props to Dad for your anonymous comments on my blogs; I'm sure no one knew that "I drink in Starshine's words like water in the desert" was written by a blood relative. I've learned by watching my aunt Yoyo and cousin Aletia that there's no integrity in whining; I'm working on it.

I love my work. I love investigating derby girls and ranting about breast milk cheese and looking up synonyms for ... synonym. And I couldn't do any of it without JG, the sexiest man I've ever met, who gives me time to write and designs beautiful books for me and lets me make fun of him in print.

Stone and Dash, I'm sorry; I blew it with your baby books. Just couldn't keep up. But you'll always have this book to describe what our lives were like when you were young: Wobbling weekly between surprising and predictable. Teetering daily between fun and frazzled. And just on the edge of perfect.

Fellas, Please!
Don't Go!

(I) ADMIT THAT FOR a moment, it sounded lovely — the perfect antidote to an evening of thumping, wailing, and being carelessly beaten with phallic weapons.

I had just been reading startling new research that shows the male gender is an endangered species. Scientists say copious hormone-tweaking chemicals in our air, food, and water are "feminizing" fellas around the globe, and up and down the ladder of the animal kingdom, from fish to polar bears to human men.

The report, published by the British chemical watchdog CHEMTrust, cites a surge of hermaphrodite toads, deer with deformed antlers, bald eagles and porpoises who can't reproduce, and male alligators with high estrogen levels. Folks, it's crazy out there.

Perhaps most alarming are the study's implications for people: The global ratio of boy-to-girl births is shifting inexplicably toward girls, and boys born to mothers with high levels of "gender bending" chemicals like phthalates and PCBs are more likely to have smaller penises, undescended testicles, and — oh, dear — a preference for playing with dolls and tea sets.

None of which is remotely funny, of course.

Except that it is. A little bit. Granted, if the opposite were happening and females were being "masculinized" into oblivion, women would be marching on Washington (holding hands, wearing hot pink ribbons, and, okay, maybe crying a little) in outrage. But it's the reversal of traditional roles that makes this crisis just the tiniest bit amusing.

Long have men been our species' protectors and warriors — the ones who do the threatening, not the threatened. And long have males been the very standard of "mankind," the basic "everyman," not the fully loaded model at risk of losing its, ahem, trim package.

But what if they do?

I confess I was firing on both X chromosomes when I began pondering this question on a recent night. My ovaries and I had jammed up and hunkered down for a cozy, quiet evening of wrapping presents by the fire. I was draping bubble bath and flower pots in sparkly gift tags and curling ribbon when the testosterone hit the fan.

Reasoning that this was a good time and place for a lightsaber battle, my irrepressibly male offspring and their hairy-chested father proceeded to jump, dive, and wail around me, accidentally whacking me in the back with a hefty plastic rapier and then giggling (yes, all three of them) during my stern but moot lecture on the inappropriateness of Jedi play in the house. That's when it occurred to me that — the toxic chemical-induced rapid mutation of our evolution notwithstanding — a world with less testosterone might be quite tolerable.

Less violence. Less mess. And the billowy silence of a sleepy Sunday afternoon would almost never be punctured with the words, "THROW, YOU IDIOT! THEY'RE UP 14 POINTS!"

But of course, in all seriousness, this mass un-manning of the planet's beasts must be halted. Biologically speaking, males can't go extinct without everyone going extinct and, frankly, the world wouldn't be much fun without them.

Because when they're not trouncing on my personal femme-bubble, I really do love men. I love their straight lines and deep voices. I love how they spend less time pondering and more time doing, and how they use their ears more than their mouths. Mostly I love the intriguing way they look at us women, their affinity for our finer details, their unabashed fascination with our femininity.

And I'll just say for the record that the idea of shrinking penises does not delight me. Still … I could stand it if their lightsabers were a little smaller.

Derby Dames

I WAS PRETTY SURE I was bitchin'. Dope on a rope. Wicked hip. I was fairly certain I had "badass" scrawled all over me. Then last week I met the roller derby chicks.

Half-scrambling, half-gliding around a no-frills rink in a concealed corner of Earl Warren Showgrounds, the Mission City Brawlin' Betties learned me that there's cool — and then there's roller-derby cool. And while I may take the occasional lap around the former, I will never so much as accidentally roll downhill into the latter. That's cooler than a polished concrete flat track in the shade. That's cool on wheels.

I'm no slouch on skates. An only (lonely) child, I spent entire Hollywood weekends shooting the moon in hot pink denim. So when a couple of girlfriends told me they were trying out for Santa Barbara's new roller derby team, I strutted over to check it out.

Invented in the 1930s, roller derby is a full-contact

sport in which knee-padded, hot-pants'd gals race each other around an oval track at break-bone speed, trying to block opponents from passing them. It was huge in the '70s, selling out arenas like Madison Square Garden, and has enjoyed a recent revival, with more than 75 leagues across the country.

What's not to love? I fell hard for the derby dames. Magenta satin bra straps beneath wife-beater tanks. Polka-dot short shorts atop fishnet stockings. Sparkly red helmets and argyle skull-and-crossbones knee socks. Mee-*yow*.

Then there are the flirty-aggro nicknames. Ranging in age from 20 to 41, the Betties are known as Viva Violence, Danger Kitty, Nurse Perverse. There's a tall redhead called Cherry Napalm. My friend, a diabetic, skates as Lo-Blo SugGrr.

"Everybody out there has fun hair colors and tattoos," said Lo-Blo, who joined up for the exercise. Burning up to 600 calories per hour, they do squats, jumps, barrel rolls, and Superman slides — all with old-school shoe skates on the ends of their impossibly toned legs.

"It's a tough game to play. There's sort of a brutal aspect to it," admitted Stray Cat, a PTA mom who plays for the Central Coast Roller Derby in Paso Robles. She's trained more than 100 derby girls, including a few from northern Santa Barbara County. "When you first start, there's the fear aspect of, 'Am I gonna knock a tooth out?' But once you've fallen a few times, it's like, 'Eh, no big deal.'"

Cat swears derby offers an "intoxicating" combo of camaraderie and confidence. "It feels like being in a very positive girl gang," she said, "a cross between a sorority and a fight club."

In Santa Barbara, the new recruits — alternately called "Baby Betties" and "fresh meat" — pant through wheeled calisthenics while pitiless, pig-tailed coach Dita de los Muertos bellows at them: "Don't look at your feet, you'll fall! Hey, pink helmet, I saw that! Head up!"

The veterans scrimmage in preparation for a Visalia bout on Saturday (check their Facebook page for local match info). Every lap or two, there's a fall and a pileup of bodies clacking and "oof"-ing as they hit the pavement.

I'm told the chick in the star helmet is the "jammer," and her job is to lap the rest of the pack. I have no idea what's going on, but by the end, the dames' once-white tanks are baseball-cleat filthy, their faces flushed, their clothes soaked with sweat.

Staring in awe from the sidelines, I'm not sweaty. Not even warm. And worst of all — now certain I could never summon the quad strength or quash the wussiness required to roll with the Betties — I find I'm not even within slapping distance of cool.

Book Club's Dramatic Chapter

I T WAS MORNING when the email arrived, its subject line blaring like a Helvetica horn: "Emergency Book Club Meeting Tonight." I hadn't drained my first cup of coffee, and now I didn't need to; there are few five-word phrases that set my adrenaline surging like this one.

It's a laughable notion, I realize. What sort of event spurs a frantic gathering of book group members? An abominable mis-casting for the movie version of *The Glass Castle?* A global embargo of pinot grigio?

But the Emergency Book Club Meeting is not something to be taken lightly. In six years, our literature-loving girl gang has called just three of these urgent rallies, each time for a life-altering predicament affecting one of our members and thoroughly outraging the rest of our close-knit sisterhood.

"Ladies," the most recent email began, "one of our own is facing a crisis situation and could use all the support and love we can offer." The crisis: a cheating husband. More specifically, a self-involved man-child who navigated through his midlife crisis by using his wilson as a compass.

The affair was clichéd, but the pain it inflicted was fresh and crude and needed tending.

Like Wonder Woman getting a distress signal from the Justice League's Trouble Alert computer, we sprung to action, hiring sitters, calling in sick at work, and stocking up on trusty trauma lube: pizza, wine, and ice cream. We gathered in a familiar living room where we've discussed Neil Gaiman and debated Roald Dahl. A room where we've had tea parties and baby showers.

We hugged, we poured, we sat — and we listened. Listened to the sickening When, the cruel How, and the heart-wrenching Why of the duplicity. And then the shocking Who: his wife's close, longtime friend.

Our double-duped friend was in shock. In pain. Incensed. We empathized, nodding and blinking back tears, because that's what women do. And then we spoke. All of us. Women who'd been cheated on, and those who some day might. Married women, single, divorced.

We made dates, filling up her calendar with promising plans. We pondered feng shui, urging her to buy new sheets and even rearrange the bedroom furniture. (It's supposed to really help. What do we know?) We told stories of philandering fathers, and boyfriends who said they weren't married.

"They do stupid things," said a gal whose spouse once strayed.

There was nothing we didn't discuss. No detail — no appendage — too small for our verbal scrutiny.

"Are they just all sucky?" I asked, exasperated, at one point.

"They're all sucky some of the time," replied one woman, who seemed to know what she was talking about.

We tried to be mature about the situation. We really did. We reminded her that love's hard, but life's long. We applauded her strength and clear thinking. And we hoped aloud that the cads' tryst felt good enough to allay their shame when the town finds out they're selfish twat-wads. Which we will ensure it does. (Hey, even Wonder Woman had to use her Amazonian berserker rage from time to time.)

Our book group is bound by more than a bent for best-selling fiction. We're partners in this page-turning drama we call life — and we don't like stories with crappy endings.

I'm not sure what will come of my friend's marriage. For all her husband's recent treachery, he's a smart guy. After coming clean about his affair, he made this astute confession to a buddy:

"I'm terrified of Book Club."

Is Waxing Waning?

IMES ARE LEAN. Money's tight. Something's gotta give. Surveys show women are cutting back on their beauty regimens to save dollars: painting their own nails, giving up facials, and stocking up, alas, on Clairol Root Touch-Up in Medium Golden Blonde.

"The economy," one of my girlfriends confessed, "is wreaking havoc on my nails and hair."

But not all hair.

I'm always amused at how women's pubic hair styles change with the times. In the '70s, the pages of *Playboy* were overgrown with va-jungles. Today the centerfolds look like nursing mothers up top and nine-year-old girls below. Skin, as they say, is in.

Gals of all ages seem to favor the Brazilian wax, which cannot be explained adequately without violating obscenity laws. But I'll try: The waxer removes every flipping follicle on the waxee's, um, undercarriage, up her backside, and anything (or everything) she wants taken off in front. Landing strip. Triangle. Cougar paw. Or need-a-muff naked.

Since fashion spins in cycles, one has to wonder: How soon before the pube pendulum swings back from bare to bushy? What will it take to end the trend toward hairless hoo-hahs?

I wondered if the economic downturn might do the trick. Brazilian waxes cost from $45-$90, and with disposable razors at under a buck, it feels profligate to pay a stranger to tear out your short ones at the root. In fact, it gives a whole new meaning to "rip off."

So I asked women all around the country if they were shaving costs off their budget by forgoing their monthly waxing. Indeed, women are cutting back on beauty rituals in Pennsylvania and Washington. They're doing it in Los Angeles and New York. But they're not necessarily doing it south of the equator.

It turns out that unlike a dye job, French manicure, or beloved massage, the bikini wax is one of those grooming splurges that some women cannot — will not — live without.

"I'd probably grow out my fro and skip the pedi before giving up the bikini wax," said a friend of mine who's been getting them for 20-plus years. "I just can't deal with hair there."

Another friend gave up her every-three-weeks waxing appointment but found she, er, couldn't hack it. "I tried, but I can't live without it," she said. "I'll just have to give up my housekeeper."

Really? It seems there's more than fashion — or

finance — fueling the fuss to be fuzz-free.

Alisa Bowman, who pens the marriage blog ProjectHappilyEverAfter.com, first got waxed two years ago as a surprise for her husband. "But I got completely hooked," she said. "It's just incredibly sexy to look at — and no amount of feminism can bring me to say that about my former woolliness. It's also a lot more sensitive. It has completely changed my sex life."

There's a lot of loyalty between women and their waxers. It's a fact: Where there's pain, and privates, there's bonding.

"I have relationships with these women," said waxer Nina Lafuente, who's been offering discounts to longtime clients faced with financial cutbacks. "Women, we're cool with each other. We like to take care of one another."

Esthetician Jamie Sprovieri said the recession hasn't affected her business at all. "In the Great Depression, the beauty industry went fairly unscathed," she said. "In times of crisis, people will do any little thing that makes them feel better: buying a tube of lipstick or taking a yoga class or getting your bikini waxed. It won't break the bank, and it makes you feel more confident."

She herself still gets regular waxes. And don't expect her to stop any time soon: "My husband is Brazilian."

Every Girl
Needs a Gay

THERE'S A MAN I meet for enchanting lunch dates. We giggle and taste each other's food. He stands up when I enter the room, and looks me frankly in the eyes. He's inexcusably handsome, laugh-out-loud funny, and whip-smart.

And when I leave for our rendezvous — wearing a smile, a flirty dress, and a spritz of mango body splash — my husband always comments, "Wow. *Who* are you having lunch with again?" When I answer, he says, "Oh! Have fun."

You see, my delicious date is gay. Gay as they come. Dresses-better-than-I-do gay. Big-fan-of-chick-flicks gay. I fancy myself the Grace to his Will. The Madonna to his Rupert. (But not the Carrie to his Stanford. He's not *that* gay.)

Apparently I am a fag hag. But I find the term tasteless-times-two, so I go by the gentler, more fashionable "fruit fly." (The zeitgeist now also allows for "lesbros," or straight men who covet the company of lesbians. A column for another time, no doubt.)

Lots of my girlfriends have cherished friendships with gay men, and the gay part isn't incidental. These guys are not "girlfriends with penises." There's something about the breezy straight gal/gay guy dynamic that makes other friendships feel like hard labor.

Some say it's a shared love of drama. Others admit they feel hipper-by-proximity when they sashay into a party on the arm of an out-and-proud-er.

But here's the coolest part of having a gay boyfriend: There's no sexual tension (is he hot for me?) like there is with straight male friends, and there's no competition (is she hotter than me?) like there is with straight female friends. The relationship is miraculously relaxed.

Our gays make us feel attractive — without feeling hunted. "Isn't it nice sometimes," asks a woman I know, "when your boobies are admired and appreciated in ways that are less...leering?"

Plus, we share an edginess that comes from living in a "man's world."

"No matter how well enculturated they are," explains my homosexual honey, "gay men still grew up on the outside, which often gives them a perspective that's either bitter or humorous." Both, please!

And the unbridled honesty. Oof.

"My boys," says a gal with lots of gay pals, "have the balls (figuratively and literally) to tell me the stuff my female friends won't, like, 'You look fat in that' or, 'He's totally not into you.'"

Another asked her gay friend to teach her how to properly fellate a fella. "He instructed me on a bottle," she says. "It was informative, fun, and very, very useful. I still use what he told me."

Still others brag that their gay friends are great listeners, gifted fashion advisers, and are happy to share an evening watching Janet Jackson videos on YouTube.

"On a weekly basis, I talk to my gay more than anyone else I know," says one woman. "When I told him I was considering moving to another state to find a job, he said, 'Oh, no. There will be no moving.' It made me feel loved."

To be fair, there are downsides to the relationship. Some ladies complain that their gay friends are capable of summoning a level of bitchy at which we gals can only tremble in awe.

"My gay has made me cry," says a friend of mine. "He says, 'I just can't not be snarky! It's who I am!' Gays. Always with the snarky."

Case in point: A woman I know bragged that her gay confidant of 30 years is the most thoughtful, generous, nonjudgmental gentleman she knows. Then she asked him, out of curiosity, why he liked her.

"Because," he deadpanned, "you're the same sex as Cher."

The Mythical Cougar

ARRIED, MID THIRTIES, and bereft of an urban feline's riveting "Rowrrrr," I'm no cougar. But I watched the season premiere of TV Land's reality show *The Cougar,* a *Bachelor*-style series in which a foxy 40-year-old divorcée and mother of four is wooed by 20 hairless, pec-flexing beauhunks.

Stacy, the giggly Barbie-clone from Arizona, whittles down the batch by literally "kissing off" each episode's winners and losers — a dweeb who told her "You're under arrest; you stole my heart" got to stay while a dork who made a crude sexual joke was shown the door. Another kept blurting, "I have my own house!" as though the statement alone were an aphrodisiac. They were play-acting at being men.

Still, I watched. I watched because I wanted to see the mythical Cougar dynamic in action. I have no trouble picturing what my cougar friends bluntly call the "no-strings-attached athletic sex." In fact, let's all take a moment to picture it now together, just because we can.

It's the hook-up that I get stuck on. The part where the mammogram-aged vixen and the Halo-playing meathead lock eyes and fall in lust. In *The Cougar*, it happens when Stacy meets her wide-eyed, faux-hawked, hooting suitors.

"This is a dream come true," she says. Which is funny to me. Because it looks like a nightmare.

I've heard some great arguments for dating a younger man. "He probably doesn't have a mortgage, ex-wife, and three kids, and can't really even comprehend what all that will do to him," explains a girlfriend who knows from experience. With or without their clothes on, they're enthusiastic. Plus they have that yummy newish skin.

But some of my forty-ish gal pals say the call to cougarhood is exaggerated.

"I think there are more young pups who'd like to believe women want boy toys," says a friend, "than there are women who find them appealing."

It's true. Young dudes are all six-pack and no savoir-faire. They're jumpy and cocksure and can't quote from *The Princess Bride* or hum a Violent Femmes song. What are you supposed to do with that?

"I like a fella with history, stories, opinions, perspective, rationale, complexities," says a friend of cougaring age. "I like someone with a few scars who's been through stuff. These [cougar-bait] boys are so fresh and squeaky clean — what 'stuff' have they been through that could possibly hold this jaded old lady's attention?"

Stacy-the-Cougar says young men fit perfectly with her lifestyle. But with four kids and a successful real-estate job, I have to assume she means as a sitter.

"I got hit on by a 22-year-old," confesses another career gal I know. "We fooled around but I needed to guide him. He was like Bambi on new legs. There just wasn't any wisdom yet."

Even my Cougar-and-Proud girlfriends say there are downsides to dating the boys of Generation Y. "They can be flaky if a better offer comes along," says one, "and you have to learn the kids' abbreviations so you can communicate via text, because you'll never get an actual phone call."

No, thanks. I like the patience that guys my age possess. They don't seem like they're going to explode if they don't fulfill their biological urges within 10 minutes of paying the check. They know they can dip into a reservoir of skills, talents, and experience to charm a lady slowly, and deeply — like cracking a safe by listening for the soft "clicks" rather than trying to pry it open with a crowbar.

Okay. I think I found my "Rowrrrr" ...

Welcome to the Gun Show

I SPEND MY LIFE hunting for exercise in disguise — activities that will hasten my heart rate and tone my tail feathers without me much noticing. Too aggro for yoga, too wussy for … well, anything that hurts, I need to be tricked into fitness. I need it to just sort of happen while I'm living my otherwise delightful and not especially active life.

Which is why my friend Margaret suggested we spend a nice evening chasing one another around in the dark, trying to kill each other dead.

Margaret is not a scary person. She's an erudite English professor and cookie-baking mommy who happens to have a jones for laser combat. For months, she has been begging me to join her at Motionz laser tag in Santa Maria for a weekly Lasercise night (wha … ?) and when I run out of excuses, I gather my up-for-anything gal pals Kate and Kalai and bite the bullet. Or rather nibble the bright red beam.

On the drive up, we giggle and snort as Margaret briefs us Spandex-clad suburbanites on Lasercise procedure. Clad in high-tech, sensor-laden vests and wielding bad-ass light-launching weaponry, we will do calisthenics and then play back-to-back laser-tag games in Motionz's two-story indoor war zone. The object is simple: Shoot people, and don't get shot.

To drown out the self-doubt smoldering in our guts (guns? really?), we crack jokes about the task at hand. When we hear there's no running allowed, Kalai quips, "Aha, so it's like playing by the pool." When we learn that code names will be assigned to us — Dark Sovereign, Venom, Dr. Doom — Kate pouts, "I just know I'm gonna get something fat."

Margaret insists the game's a stress buster: "It's like an odd form of meditation. When you're in there, no other worries can creep into your mind. All you can think about is not getting hit."

What do you lose if you get hit? I ask. "Self-esteem."

We arrive late. We've missed the group stretches and lunges; I like the place already. We suit up in the black-lit "vesting room," where our eyeballs, teeth, and the startling amount of lint on our über-cute stretchpants glow eerily. Inside the dark labyrinth, colored lights flash and haunting techno music thumps.

"When are they gonna release the lions?" Kate mutters.

One minute the grandmotherly owner of the place is guiding me through the arena with the hospitality of a bed-and-breakfast proprietor ("Here's the blue base. See that green light? Shoot it. Good!"). The next she's coldly blasting me in the chest.

They're hardcore, this Motionz militia. One fellow wearing fatigues and an unneighborly scowl seems to think I'm a threat to his freedom and stalks me like prey. He's the kind of soldier who stealthily creeps up ramps and squats behind crates to pick off his enemies (read: humanity at large), all the while guarding his precious sensors from sight.

I'm the kind, it turns out, who shrieks and cackles every time I get shot — which is every three or four seconds — and runs kamikaze-style through my friends' vicious laser crossfire howling, "Leave me alone, you trigger-happy bitches! I'm just here for my gluuuuuutes!"

I'm hit more than 100 times that night, coming in last place.

"Don't you feel cleansed?" Margaret asks when it's over.

In truth, I feel gritty. And exhausted. And ... sweaty! Holy fat-burner, Rambo, I really did get exercise!

Margaret got a bloody knuckle that night. Kalai bruised her elbow. The next day, I was sore, too: My face and sides hurt from laughing so much. Turns out I've got a new favorite workout. But it's not laser tag. It's laughing my ass off.

LIFE, OR THEREABOUTS

The Height
of My Career

(I) 'M NOT A GINORMOUS person. Not hulking. Not alpine. I couldn't, like, take down Ann Coulter in a cage fight, although I'd really enjoy trying. But at five-foot-ten and prone to heels, I'm on the lanky side.

Still, I'm astonished how many readers meet me and make this exact comment:

"Wow. You look so much ... shorter in your photo."

I get it all the time. As if it were a perfectly rational thing to say. As if they believed my column mugshot were actual size, and the rest of my body should be six, seven inches tall.

"You're big," people inform me. "We thought you were this petite little thing." They don't say it in a "Wow, life is full of fun surprises" kind of way. They say it like it's disconcerting. Like I've forever destroyed their ability to trust themselves.

One woman actually held up my book, pointed to the

author photo on the back and said to her friend, "Look at her! That's a small person, I'm sorry."

The first few times it happened, I let it go. Chuckled, shrugged, tried not to feel like a freak. Maybe squatted a bit, trying to slowly, surreptitiously shrink down to the size folks picture me to be. The size they really, really want me to be.

But it happens so often these days that I can't help but wonder: From whence does this assumption spring?

I like to think they have me pegged as one of those feisty little firecrackers like Dr. Ruth, Rhea Perlman, or Reese Witherspoon, who make up in attitude what they lack in altitude. ("I'm about as tall as a shotgun," Truman Capote was known to say, "and just as noisy.")

But what if it's something else? What if I simply seem smaller in print: inconsequential, trifling?

It's always surprising to learn that a favorite actor — an action hero or romantic leading man — has to stand on a soapbox to look a female costar in the kisser; we tend to think of big stars as big dudes. It follows, then, that readers who think I'm a teeny-tiny woman may well consider me an itty-bitty writer.

It's not untrue, actually. I have a penchant for zooming in on the small stuff, click-clacking out whole columns on speeding tickets, sex tapes, and a personal body-piercing incident that's best forgotten. And I confess that when you're as tall and uncoordinated as I am, the act of navel-gazing can be both painful and unsightly.

But to me, writing should eschew the grandiose and illuminate life's niggly bits. It should remind us that we're all sort of smallish in the greater scheme of things. And it should convince us that — petite or prodigious, stocky or slight — we're far more alike than different, coping with the same frustrations and insecurities, buoyed by similar hopes and humor. It should make us feel deeply, mercifully understood.

Clearly you can't judge a scribe's stature by her stories. I'm a full foot taller than literary giant Margaret Mitchell. I tower over best-sellers J.K. Rowling, Danielle Steele, and my personal hero, Erma Bombeck. I've even got an inch or two on O. Henry and F. Scott Fitzgerald (though Michael Crichton and Maya Angelou both dwarf me).

In showbiz they say there are no small parts, only small actors. Could it be there are no short stories, only short authors? And no tall tales, just tall tellers? It's an idea worth exploring, but I have to stop typing now.

I'm short on space.

Doing the Right Thing

HEY SAY GUILT is a great motivator, but I'm unconvinced. If it were true — if disgrace and penitence could spur a gal to stand up and set things right — then I wouldn't be lying here, curled around my atrophying wallet in a shade-grown, grass-fed, phosphate-free paralysis.

I'm lame with eco-shame.

Do I read too much? Do I pay too much attention? Am I the only one confused and incapacitated by knowing the fiendish ways that every product on the market will impact our health, environment, and the progress of global human rights? Pesticides, PVCs, bioengineering. I'm afraid to consume anything for fear I might ingest *E. coli,* support sweatshops, or single-handedly deplete a rain forest.

I'm not one of those "let someone else figure out global warming; I loves me some Styrofoam" people, I swear I'm not. I'm conscientious-ish. I buy organic milk, free-range eggs, fair-trade coffee. I pack my kids' lunches in re-purposed hummus tubs instead of landfill-bound, petroleum-based sandwich baggies. I confess I still don't know what "sustainable" means, but I compost kitchen scraps for garden mulch. I even lease solar panels for my roof.

It's not enough, though. And we all know it. Having spent years dreading the confounding "paper or plastic" quiz at the end of a grocery run (you know there's no right answer, right? And that no matter what you say, you're going to Hell), I bought cute, reusable shopping bags. But they were too cheap to be as attractive as they are, and now I can't shake the feeling they were stitched by a nimble-fingered, factory-imprisoned boy named Rashid in Uzbekistan. I'm sorry, Rashid, I'm trying. I'm trying!

It's depressing to realize one lacks the mental capacity to shop responsibly. Conscientious consumption turns out to be an AP calculus problem that gums up my remedial-math mind and leaves me randomly filling in bubbles on the Scantron: Um ... renewable energy good? High-fructose corn syrup bad?

Is it better to buy a new fuel-efficient car, or pack your gas-guzzler full of carpoolers? Should you support the city's new eco-upright market? Or protest its owner's anti-union practices and public stance against universal health care?

Gain two points if you eschew pesticides. Lose two points if you squander fuel by driving all the way across town to buy chemical-free root vegetables. Gain one point if they're from a locally owned business. Lose a point if it packages each parsnip individually.

I bought a book called *The Better World Shopping Guide* at Chaucer's. It was the worst thing I ever did. The book grades more than 1,000 companies on their environmental and social impact. My son likes to go through it and tell me how our chocolate is "slave-free" but our mayonnaise is made by a "corporate villain" who "continues to do business in Burma." Neither of us knows where Burma is.

The more I read, the less I know. When *Newsweek* names McDonald's one of the nation's greenest corporations, you know society's criteria have become a-jumble. Things used to be simpler. Not long ago, the words "dolphin-safe" were all you had to know about seafood. Now, how do you choose a healthy, humane, can't-I-just-eat-my-fish-in-peace piece of salmon anymore, for carp's sake?

I like to think that normal people — people without my persnickety A-student personality — are content and even proud to make "lesser evil" choices and stick to them. But not me. I want to do it right. I want to hold up my end.

But since I'm afraid to go shopping anymore, I'll just sit here and eat the only thing in my house that doesn't seem to be triggering the end of the world. If I can't be guilt-free, at least I can be "slave-free."

What Are You Running From?

THIS TOWN IS a runner's rapture: Ribbons of scenery-skirted sidewalks, a surplus of sunshine and the shotgun start of an organized race being fired nearly every time you lace up your ASICS.

Yes, folks here like to huff and lope over endless miles of hills and plains. Glistening provocatively in tiny nylon shorts, they enjoy opening up the throttle on their miraculous, machine-like bodies and blissing out to the meditative rhythms of their feet and heart thumping in tandem, their breath chugging staccato, allegrissimo...

All of which begs the question, I think:

What is wrong with you people?

Long have I applauded and issued wow-good-for-yous when friends — in increasing numbers — tell me they've taken up running and are training for marathons and triathlons. It's good to get healthy, after all. To have hobbies. To set goals.

But no more. It's starting to feel like a plot. A conspiracy to overthrow good sense, to punish ourselves and to make us all have those weird bulbous calfs. And I just won't be a party to that.

Let me admit right off the bat that there is nothing about running that appeals to me. I won't even break into a trot unless someone crazy is chasing me.

From where I sit (which I do often), the sport looks like this: monotony + pounding + ugly shoes. And no amount of endorphins or sanctioned carb-loading can balance that grim equation. So on the runners' sanity continuum, I may be unable to accurately gauge the precise location of the line between "healthy" and "stark, raving deranged."

But I did a little research. Do you know what kinds of products are marketed to runners? Knee braces and night splints. Heart monitors and pepper spray. Clip-on strobes and blister shields. There's even something called Unisex Body Glide Anti-Friction. Is this a fitness routine, folks, or an (*ouch!*) torture scene from *Casino Royale*?

To be fair, I have no empirical evidence that training for a marathon is painful. Like the way I'm not sure if sticking one's tongue in an electrical outlet is painful, but I'm unlikely to try it.

I know, I know. Our bodies are amazing. Powerful. Resilient. It's wonderful! But some of us can appreciate that fact without pushing them to their breaking point. Some of us are plenty proud when we are able to finish our dinner after ordering our Thai food "medium" spicy instead of our usual "mild." Talk about a rush! Plus you get that same rosy runners' glow on your cheeks without the inevitable knee surgery.

I don't begrudge my buddies who take joy in the occasional jog. It must be nice to get exercise anytime you want — no doubles partner, gym membership or Pilates ring required.

It's the harder-farther-faster folks whose motives I question. I have several friends who have completed the Ironman. That means they willingly — nay, eagerly — swam two-and-a-half miles (Milpas Street isn't that long), biked 112 miles (Santa Barbara County isn't that long) and then, what the heck, ran a marathon when they were done.

Look, I'm no expert. I can't say for sure that athletes who enter the Ironman are clinically insane. But I can say this: If those people were chasing me, I would run.

Prime-Time Promises

I GREW UP IN Hollywood. More specifically, on the set of *General Hospital,* where my dad was a propman. It was an odd place for a girl to come of age. The days were long, the pace was pokey, and I had to be impossibly quiet all the time, literally skittering up into the rafters whenever the child-loathing executive producer marched into the studio unexpectedly.

But there was a part of it I relished: seeing firsthand how phony everything was. On the TV screen at home, Port Charles looked hyper-real and beautiful. But on set, it was so obviously fake. And creepy.

The plastic food was brushed with water to make it glisten. The hunky stars — Rick Springfield and John Stamos — were spackled with spongy, unskin-like makeup. The fog was dry ice. The wine was grape juice. And the front of each character's stately home was a flimsy plywood facade that wobbled if you leaned on it.

Throughout several sitter-less summers, I became a

connoisseur of these idiot-box illusions. Which makes it all the more embarrassing that I recently got sucked into Tinseltown's manipulation machine, bamboozled by the promise of prime-time prominence.

A friend in the biz was passing around my book to industry nabobs when a reputable TV producer reportedly fell sick-in-love with my "voice" and asked me to "take a meeting."

I was suspicious. People cheat and steal to get meetings like this. They don't just happen; they don't come to you. But who was I to argue with the man's money, I mean his creative vision?

"You are terrific," he told me, waving my book in his hand. "Terrific. I see a sitcom here."

"You do?" I asked, wondering how anyone could make a sitcom out of a book of columns.

"I'm looking at 8:30 Tuesday nights on CBS," he said.

"You are?!" I asked.

The conversation was a dream. Until I off-handedly mentioned my kids.

"You got kids?" he said.

How could he not know this? Half the columns in my book are about being a parent. Even if he had never opened the book (dear god, had he never opened the book?), it says "mother of two" on the cover ...

But the sweet talk came so fast. The names of it-guy directors and it-gal actresses. The comparisons to *Sex and the City*. The email crowing, "I'm ordering the EMMY now!" Once, during a phone conference, I tuned out and began fantasizing about what kind of obscure '80s candy I would insist upon having in my dressing room.

In truth, I tuned out quite often during conversations with the Men Who Would Make Me Famous. Because I never really understood what they were saying. Propmen perpetrate their illusions with double-face tape; television execs do it with doublespeak. My friend Matt Allen, who wrote the Reese Witherspoon movie *Four Christmases,* tried to explain the lingo to me:

"'I left word' really means I didn't do anything," he said. "I may or may not have called, probably not. 'He read it. He liked it' means he did not like it. 'He read it. He doesn't get it' means your guy didn't get the reaction he wanted and he's pissed, if you want to know the truth."

I did want to know the truth. And eventually I figured it out: They didn't know how to make a sitcom out of a book of columns. Which is just as well. Even a soundstage baby can be stupefied by TV's razzle-dazzle lure.

If Hollywood ever wants me again, it knows where to find me. I'll be hiding in the rafters.

Dazzling Dollhouse

LIFE, ONLY SMALLER

LONG BEFORE I OWNED a big velvet couch, I owned an itty-bitty one. Years before I could sweep my front porch with a broom, I could dust it off with a fingertip. And decades before my dining room sparkled under a ponderous chandelier, it glowed under a pee-wee one, about two inches long.

I had a dollhouse. A dazzling, one-of-a-kind dollhouse that my father built for me. A blue, two-story Victorian with an Astroturf lawn, white popsicle-stick fence, and working lights — and switches — in every room.

My dad's a woodcarver, and quite a craftsman. The way he remembers it, I approached him one day with this oh-so-casual remark: "Grandma said you could make me a dollhouse. You couldn't do that, could you?"

And the game was on.

He called it my "tiny mansion" and worked on it most of the year in his garage, in secret. I recall with breathtaking precision the moment I first saw it: French doors and balconies, old-fashioned wallpaper, buzzing doorbell. A wooden cutting board slid out from the kitchen counter. My initials were carved above the front door in scroll letters.

My dad's a joy to me. He's smart and funny and there when I need him. But if he'd never done another kind thing for me — ever in my life — this would have been enough.

It was a little girl's fantasia. Like Dorothy's house flattening the Wicked Witch of the East, it crushed my interest in lesser playthings like Fashion Plates and Shrinky Dinks. Easy Bake Oven? Meh.

Life in miniature is enchanting to a child. Whereas the adult world seems immense and ungraspable, sprawling and unwieldy, this pretty microcosm was tidy, inviting and self-contained. Full of delicate treasures and cottage comforts, it was a promise of glorious grown-up days to come, when I would be mistress of my own home. And have a pink claw-foot tub. Just because.

I inhabited that dollhouse. I re-arranged furniture, stocked the fridge with clay food, and snipped throw rugs from my mother's sewing scraps. I created a game room in the attic and arranged Lilliputian playing cards in diminutive games of gin. I collected errant figurines from other toy sets to erect as statues in the yard.

Through my play, I experimented with possible future vocations: Landscaper. Interior designer. Home maker. Architect.

Shortly after the mommy and daddy dolls began, um, mysteriously turning up in the pink tub together, my interests shifted. I didn't want to play house; I wanted to play music, play with friends, play with boys.

As I grew up, the dollhouse grew still. And dusty. Bulky and brimming with negligible knick-knacks, it was bumped from bedroom to spare room to storage — until I got married and finally had a home of my own to keep it in. A two-story home with French doors and a buzzing doorbell, if you must know.

For years now it's been standing in the center of my garage as my disinterested sons knock into it with their remote-control cars and stomp rockets. Smudged, dinged, and uncared for, it stands in the way of their expanding collections of scooters and drums. The lights no longer work; little combs and dishes litter its floors.

So this week, I dusted it, rearranged the furniture one last time and drove it to a women's shelter, where it just might offer refuge for the imaginations of troubled kids.

It was the right decision; even Dad was delighted. But I shed childish tears as I left it behind. How could it be that now — while living in the biggest house I've ever called home — I've finally run out of room for my first and smallest house? My favorite house. My tiny mansion.

Never Say Neverland

THE EMAIL WAS CURT, and cryptic. A *New York Post* writer wanted help on a story about the rumpus outside Michael Jackson's Santa Ynez home. His follow-up phone call was equally cloak-and-dagger: "Drive to 5225 Figueroa Mountain Road and call us when you get there."

It was the one place on this gargantuan planet that I least wanted to spend my day. I had planned several leisurely hours of writing interrupted only by 37 visits to Facebook and a long-awaited lunch with a girlfriend who makes me giggle.

But here's the truly awful thing about being a reporter: When there's something to report, you must report it. It's in the job description. It IS the job description.

So I report:

I spent 10 minutes getting ready. One minute to pack water, snacks, notepads, extra pens, sunscreen, a phone charger, laptop, and maps of the backcountry in case the roads were blocked and I had to hike in (no, of course I wouldn't really have done it, but one must go through the motions so she can say she "tried"). And the remaining nine minutes figuring out what to wear.

When covering news events, it's important to blend in with the folks you're interviewing (unlike the poor TV reporters who, when cameras rolled, had to slip into blazers and slap on smiles in the 90-plus-degree heat). But shimmying into jeans, a T-shirt, and sneakers, I realized I had no idea how to fit in among Jackson's fans. People who brave Neverland's chaos not for a paycheck or byline, but because they can't imagine NOT being there, were an utter mystery to me.

And I rather wish they still were.

Rounding the bend to the rural estate, I gasped aloud when the idyllic cow-and-pasture vistas gave way to a full mile of news satellite vans parked end to end to no end.

A full day before the superstar's family, and body, were expected at the ranch, news crews outnumbered visiting fans by at least three to one.

The sprawl emanated out from the property's stately gates, adorned with wreaths of white roses. Despite the makeshift memorial of candles, bouquets, and personal (read: creepy) letters, the mood was congenial. A couple dozen Jackson devotees and pop culture junkies took orderly turns snapping photos in front of the gate.

Some were in town for weddings or vacations and couldn't resist checking out this "once in a lifetime" event. Others were locals who trotted up in high heels on their lunch breaks.

The gates opened frequently, letting in a landscaping truck, letting out a storage truck, and allowing the guards — who were playing Jackson tunes from a stereo — to hand out bottled water to the crowd. But this was a hearty lot.

"I once waited 19-and-a-half hours in line for a ticket to see Michael Jackson in concert in Las Vegas," said Julia Sullivan, 62, of Arroyo Grande. "I just loved the way he danced. I still have my VHS tapes of 'Thriller.' I watch them all the time."

There was an exceptionally fit young woman in a bikini. An Indiana dog breeder with four leashed poodles. A couple of brooding teens in red pleather Jacko jackets. And then there was Aja Diaz of Oxnard, there for her 16th birthday. She was disappointed to discover she wouldn't be able to see Jackson's corpse.

"It kind of sucks," she explained. "That's, like, all I can say." And it truly was.

"Big, big, huge fan" Paul Barron of Bellflower was at the infamous 1984 Pepsi commercial shoot when Jackson's hair caught fire. And he visited the singer's star on the Hollywood Walk of Fame after hearing of his death.

"Time stopped," said Barron, 56. He brought his teenage granddaughter Tiffany to Neverland to pay further respect.

"All the good ones," lamented Tiffany, "are passing away."

Farrah Fawcett and Karl Malden?

"Bernie Mac and Isaac Hayes."

Cycle-wary

N OLD BIKER ADAGE says there are two kinds of motorcycle riders: those who have been down, and those who are going down.

Bikers court danger; it's part of the thrill of riding. And the axiom is their way of acknowledging the inevitable.

Spend enough time in the World of Two Wheels, though, and you become forcibly acquainted with a third category: Riders who have been down and down and down again. Knocked down and plowed down. Dragged behind trucks. Pinched between fenders. Raked across loose gravel.

My dad falls into this category — tumbles into it regularly, in fact. Dad loves biking for its "illusion of flying" but too often experiences the "actuality of flying" while hurtling through an intersection face-first. The details of his many hospital-requiring collisions congeal in my memory; sutures blend into slings blend into surgeries. But I can recall with startling accuracy the sickening feeling of hearing him say, each time, "I'm really lucky. I should have been dead."

Last week, two days after Dad's 65th birthday, an SUV plowed through a red light, busting his clavicle in two. It wasn't the first time he'd broken a clavicle. It wasn't even the first time he'd broken that clavicle. But it was the first time I resented him for making me worry so much.

The thing is, I get it. I understand the allure. I grew up on a motorcycle. Dad had me riding his 1937 Harley-Davidson Knucklehead before I could walk, my car seat strapped to the sissy bar with bungee cords. When he picked me up from grade school on his chopper, my classmates stood at the fence and watched me climb on, start the engine, and gun the accelerator before we howled off.

He adapts his bikes with a "suicide" foot clutch and jockey shift lever made from a chrome sword handle. In a word, they're bitchin'.

In college, I got a Class M license and piloted a Honda scooter around L.A. I had some near misses, frequently froze my throttle off, and could scarcely get to class when it rained. But I loved the bike's alchemic ability to turn still air into bracing, skin-whipping wind. I loved zig-zagging between clunky sedans on clogged urban arteries and parking any-flipping-where I wanted. I loved leaning my body into the bends of the road and having a roller coaster at my fingertips.

Riding a motorcycle isn't just exhilarating. It's life-affirming, like riding a bullet. With the street a menacing black blur streaming just inches beneath your feet, you're so close to danger it's intoxicating. And like any good drug, it clouds your judgment.

Once, Dad took my young son for a ride. Outfitted in a leather jacket, skull-cap helmet, and the widest smile of his life thus far, my kid cruised Santa Barbara with his bugs-in-the-teeth granddad. Days later, alone in the saddle again, Dad was clipped by a truck and dragged across pavement for a dozen feet on the mangled hog.

He was really lucky. He should have been dead. The more he wrecks, the more I fret, but I can't ask him to stop. Because the more he climbs back on, the more I realize how much he loves it.

Dad's given up other vices: drinking, smoking. He's trying to quit donuts. And this last wreck may have finally convinced him to hang up his helmet. "When it's doing more to you than it does for you, it's time to quit," he told me recently, to my shock.

Hard to imagine Dad trading the illusion of flying for the reality of living. But I sure love the image of him zooming freely into a fourth category of biker: Those who are done going down.

Gay Marriage in the Midwest

WHY IOWA KICKS CALIFORNIA'S TONED, TANNED TUSHIE

WE USED TO BE the shizzle. Remember? For decades, California was the nation's pacesetter. The birthplace of Barbie, blue jeans, and the birth control pill, the Golden State prided itself on dragging the rest of the nation into tomorrow. Or, at the very least, into Tomorrowland.

Faced with decisions like, "Shall we elect a glute-flexing cyborg as governor?" and "Should we light up the country's first medical marijuana initiative?" we grinned our laidback grins, sipped our Left Coast syrah, and said, "Sure! Why not?"

We were the heralds of "hot." The harbingers of "hip." But no more.

Last week, our high court handed over that mantle to a pot-bellied, farm-belt state called Iowa. Perhaps you've heard of it. Whereas California's Supreme Court voted to uphold a ban on gay marriage, Iowa has been marrying gays since April.

They're not the only ones. Connecticut, Maine, Massachusetts, and Vermont have given their blessings to gay nuptials, too.

But Iowa? The court's decision was unanimous, and emphatic. Stephen Colbert joked that the ruling makes sense: "There's nothing else to do in Iowa: shuck corn, drag race, pound a sixer, shuck more corn, propose to your football coach."

In fact, Iowa has a long history of defending equality. It desegregated its schools almost a century before 1954's landmark *Brown v. Board of Education*, and was one of the first states to permit interracial marriage. All of which confirms that California is now humiliatingly bass-ackward. And the heartland prairie that is Iowa — origin of the Winnebago — is wicked cool.

"They have those covered bridges!" says my friend Alex Kuisis, who drove through the state once. "And Amish people! Who isn't fascinated by Amish people?"

I went looking for more evidence that Iowa rocks. Home of Glenn Miller, John Wayne, and the guy who painted "American Gothic," the Hawkeye State boasts the esteemed University of Iowa Writers' Workshop, and the telltale Iowa Caucus.

You thought San Francisco's Lombard Street was the crookedest street in the world? That honor goes to Snake Alley in Burlington, Iowa. And the largest Danish settlement in the U.S. isn't Solvang. It's Elk Horn, Iowa. How do you like them aebelskiver?

Though Iowans grow soybeans, their tastes run toward less foo-foo fare like the Maid-Rite "loose meat" sandwich, a scoop of ground beef between two puffy, white, grease-dipped buns. Iowans swear crime rates and housing prices are low. And while the weather is bad, the people are extraordinarily good.

"We were in a gnarly tornado several years ago," recalls my Santa Barbara friend Kelly Tanowitz, who was visiting a family homestead there, "and the entire high school football team had come and cleaned up everything before we were awake the next morning."

"The people are amazing," echoes JenHolly Anderson, who grew up in Santa Ynez but fell in love with Iowa while attending college there, and moved there permanently. "I have found Iowans to be incredibly supportive, open, and kind in their interactions."

She says there are plenty of residents with conservative social views, but the state's decision to allow gay marriage is in keeping with its primary values. "It shows that Iowans care more about another individual's rights as a human being than their own political convictions."

Look, gay marriage is inevitable. All civil rights battles end badly for bigots, and this one, like those before it, is a forgone conclusion, a done deal. Or *fait accompli,* as they never ever say in Iowa.

Until then, take a cue from *The Music Man,* the corn-belt-set quintessential American musical: "What the heck, you're welcome, glad to have you with us. You really ought to give Iowa a try."

Pearly Whites

H AVING BRUNCH WITH Dr. Laura. Running naked across the 101. Reading the *News-Press*.

These are all things I'm more likely to be doing on a Sunday morning than attending church.

I'm an atheist. Not an agnostic. Not "spiritual but not religious." Just a full-blown, you-people-are-crazy, call-me-a-heathen-if-you-must atheist. I can't even get myself to capitalize the word god (so if it's upper-cased in this column, you'll know my editor feels differently).

When our first son was born, my Methodist in-laws asked if we planned to take him to church. "It's a great place to meet like-minded parents," they said.

"Unless you don't believe in god," my husband chuckled. "Then it's a place to meet unlike-minded parents."

But I did go to church — just once — earlier this year. I had heard about this cool local parish that's high on karma and low on dogma. Everyone I know who goes there is free-thinking, unpreachy, and socially conscious. And I was curious. What could make people give up a precious Sunday morning — unique to the week for its sunny, undemanding emptiness — to put on undergarments and sit on a wooden bench where they might have to think about locusts?

Plus, I'm jealous of the sense of community that church-goers enjoy. They always have babysitters on hand, and volunteers to help them move. No one wants to help an atheist move. No one wants to babysit our heretic children while we're out at our pagan parties.

So I ducked anonymously into this pretty church and slipped into an empty pew toward the back. Knowing my mouth would be closed for an hour, I withdrew two Crest whitening strips from my purse and pasted them over my teeth. Long as I was purifying my soul, why not bleach my ivories, too? A morning of self-betterment both inside and out.

But when the service started, the pastor asked his flock to introduce themselves to any new faces. Dear god.

The women behind me and beside me both leaned in and extended their hands. Not wanting to expose my peroxide-pasted pearlies, I did what any rational person would do: I pretended to drop my purse and dove toward the floor to pick it up.

"Don't you write for *The Independent*?" one said. "Hi," I mumbled, blushing, with my hand over my mouth. "Nameth Thtarthine."

"Are you alright?" she asked. They're very compassionate, these people.

I may be a sinner, but I'm no liar. "I'm whitening my

teeth," I explained. "That'th why I'm talking like thith."

"You're ... multitasking?" she said, her smile sliding down her face. Was that bad? Surely no god would want me to parade through this world with dingy dentistry.

The service was lovely. Inspiring, even. We sang "Here Comes the Sun" and people shared stories of change in their lives. For the first time, I really understood the appeal of church. Like seeing a therapist, Sunday worship is scheduled mindfulness — setting aside a small chunk of time to think about important things, to wrestle with them quietly, in a softly lit spot, so we can put them out of our heads for the rest of the week.

But I won't go back. The divinity-invoking raised my hackles, and the congregation was pushy, trying to get me to stay afterward and sign up for things. I'm not a stayer. Not a congregater. Not a signer-upper. Their program just didn't do enough to wear down my infidel enamel.

The Whitestrips, on the other hand, worked miracles.

Unforgettable Mistakes

WHAT DID YOU DO RIGHT TODAY?

O PTIMISTS THINK NEWSPAPERS exist to inform us. Cynics think they exist to allow advertisers access to our discerning eyeballs. They're both wrong. The primary purpose of a newspaper is to remind us that life is woefully, wickedly unfair. And to bring us Sudoku.

I read a story in *The Independent* not long ago that verified life's injustice: A young woman was boozing at a local watering hole when some barflies began bothering her and she decided to drive home. She was drunk, and planned to find a spot where she could park and sleep it off. But that's not what happened.

In the haze of drink, in the dark of night, she made a bad decision. She pulled onto the road and slammed head-on into another car, killing its driver — an innocent wife and mother.

It was horrendously unfair, criminally so. The young woman who caused the accident will pay millions in damages and spend at least a dozen years in jail. And after she has done those things, she'll spend her life reliving the moment she screwed up, wishing she could do it over, do it differently. Her egregious error will define her forever.

Is that fair? Probably.

But it got me thinking: It's so easy to pinpoint the wretched mistakes we make in life — and so hard to know what exactly we've done right. The results of poor decisions haunt us tangibly, in injury or shame or loss; but the results of smart choices, prudent choices, go largely unmarked.

It's impossible to know, for example, how many lives are spared when we don't drive home drunk. When we opt not to order another round. Or choose to call a cab. It's impossible to measure the success of responsible behavior; and equally impossible to ignore the flagrant results of recklessness.

So much of the feedback we get in life — and I mean direct, A+B=C feedback, not promotions or diplomas or anniversary cards — is spurred by missteps. We give in to a hot fling, we pay for it in marital damage, despite the years of fidelity that preceded it. We call our boss an ass clown, we feel the sting of lost wages and the drudge of job-hunting, regardless of how many mornings we dragged ourselves into work with a smile.

Since "bad" choices like texting while driving or taking shortcuts down dark alleys can have pronounced, life-altering results while "good" decisions like wearing a helmet and eating your vegetables merely allow us to (yawn) maintain the status quo, life is quick to floodlight our mistakes, and decades-slow to reveal our successes. Which is un-flipping-fair.

If we must bear the burden of our jumbo blunders, why can't we revel in the rapture of our not infrequent rightness? Okay, so we can't look into an alternate, Bizarro-Scrooge future and see the happy results of the many smart choices we make on a daily basis. (Ah, there's Tiny Tim! He's alive because we decided at the last minute not to plow through that yellow light after all!) But what we can do is take more credit for the good calls we make.

Today, for example, I removed a vitamin from the counter where the dog could have reached it. I remembered to turn off the coffee pot before leaving the house. I waited until I got to a stop sign to futz with my iPod. And I told my son not to climb up the pantry shelves.

Heroic? Hardly. Just a few niggling "rights" undertaken to stave off those dreaded life-defining "wrongs." Just a small inventory of the day's quiet victories to balance the louder, and inevitable, screw-ups of my life.

And that — if nothing else — is fair.

Cars Are for Banging

THERE ARE MOMENTS in life when you realize you're different from everyone else. Like fundamentally, even freakishly, different. And that you may never see things the way others do.

I feel that way when people exalt Jack Johnson (I'd yawn if I could summon the energy). Or when they confess that public speaking terrifies them (the mere sight of a podium turns me on). Or when they utter incongruous phrases like, "It's too sweet for my taste." (Wha… ?)

Those sentiments don't fit into the jigsaw puzzle that is my brain. Nor does this one: "Yikes. What happened to your car?"

I hear it a lot. When I pull into a friend's driveway, see an acquaintance at the gas station, or drive through the school drop-off line.

"Ouch. What happened to your poor car?"

It always takes me a second to figure out what they're talking about. Then I remember the sizable dent and scrape on the side of my Honda, the result of parking next to a short pole and carelessly slamming into it as I backed out. That was two years ago, and — though the sound it made was otherworldly, causing bystanders to wince and tighten their shoulders up around their earlobes — I've scarcely thought of it since. In fact, I only recall it when people gasp and offer heartfelt sympathy, as though it had happened to my face, rather than my fender.

"Oh no!" they say. "Your car!"

And here's where I figure I'm weird. Because I truly don't comprehend the concern. I can't even make myself understand it. To me, a car isn't something to be protected; it's there to protect me and anyone else brave enough to ride with me.

I'm an aggressive driver, I admit it. An impatient driver. When my husband is feeling charitable, he says I'm an artist and the road is my canvas. When I drove over a rose bush to extricate myself from a stifling parking space, causing a thick, thorny branch to lodge in my Michelin, he called me something else.

Still, I maintain my thesis: My car is not a red-carpet gown. It's a stick-shift suit of armor, a highway-rated hazmat suit, if you will. The exterior is scraped, dented, and, um, impaled so that I am not. No one blubbers when an umbrella gets wet, or a helmet gets dinged, right? If a car is damaged and its passengers intact, it means the thing is *working.*

Some folks, I know, consider their cars to be shiny, Turtle Waxed reflections of their status and style. Not me. In high school, I totaled my car. My grandfather, a sort of mechanical genius with a reverence for function and an indifference to form, kindly fixed it for me. He un-crunched the hood and affixed an old aluminum screen door where the grill had been. I drove it that way for years. My friends had a name for my coupe-turned-jalopy: the Road Warrior. It was a lesson in humility.

That's why, when I dented my Honda's hatchback by using my booted foot to slam it closed, I shrugged. That's why my son is still alive after having scratched his name into the driver's door with a rock. And that's why, when people offer their condolences and say, "I know a guy who can bang out those dents for you," I politely decline for two reasons:

One, if the finish were flawless, I'd have to be careful not to hit anything, and that's just stifling.

And two, I'm rather possessive about my latest road warrior. No one's allowed to bang this baby but me.

Where Have All the Assholes Gone?

T'S A FUTILE EXERCISE, but once in a while, I do it anyway. I indulge in a little nostalgia for things that used to be. New York Seltzer. Grunge fashion. The theme to *The Larry Sanders Show*. These things made me genuinely, stupidly happy until, like gnat carcasses, they were wiped clean from the windshield of our whizzing culture.

But when I take my deliberately slow and doubtlessly ill-advised stroll down Reminisce Road, there's something I find I miss more than anything else, something I never truly appreciated until it was gone — the asshole.

Have you noticed it doesn't exist anymore? In bygone eras, they were everywhere you looked. The guy who refused to leave a tip, the boss who dumped work on your desk at 5:15, the driver who pulled in front of you and slammed on her brakes.

Different generations had different names for these loathsome blights on common courtesy. Shakespeare called them knaves, pignuts, clotpoles. Early Americans denounced them as scalawags and reprobates. Your grandpa may have cursed the neighborhood lout, heel, or cad.

Me, I've always just called them jerks. Until now, that is. Enlightenment, it seems, has purged the planet of jackasses. Obliterated all the SOBs. Annihilated the bastards. Because the more we learn about human psychology, the more we find that people have legitimate — and even, sigh, excusable — reasons for behaving inconsiderately.

Remember, for example, the neighbor who berated you for playing your music too loudly at 9 p.m. on a Friday night? Turns out she's not a malevolent shrew; she's just going through a bad divorce. You know that guy who insults you every time you run into him around town? He's not actually an arrogant turd; he's just insecure from a childhood trauma. Even the client who hired you and then wouldn't return your calls after you completed the job is not the vicious tool you thought he was. He simply suffers from Integrity Deficit Disorder or some such forgivable malady.

Current compassion asks us to absolve all tyrants, pardon all villains, and accept that even Darth Vader had fair cause to be cranky from time to time. It's true: No one wants to be mislabeled by a sanctimonious observer who lacks the crucial backstory to judge us fairly.

But doing away with the "dirtbag" designation carries its own risk. Back when the classification really meant something, it was a decent deterrent to tactless behavior.

Now that the label won't stick, we're giving genuine sleazebags license to abuse us at will: "Don't bother scooping up the dog poop, darling. They'll just assume we were molested by priests in our youth and that'll be that." Thus the ultimate irony: By stifling our instinct to identify meanie-weenies, we may, in fact, be creating them.

More importantly and less profoundly, though, I just miss screaming "Flickwad!" out the car window. I pine for the days when I could sweep strangers into sordid but simple little slots without pausing to consider the psychological roots of their abominable actions and atrocious attitudes. When someone sends a bitchy email to a teacher and then carbon copies all the other class parents just because she can, I resent having to invest the time to ponder whether she's had a hug today.

Empathy, feh. It's exhausting being sensitive. And while I realize that saying so makes me precisely the sort of you-know-what I've been castigating all along, I think I'm ready to wear the word with pride. Somebody's got to.

I'm bringing asshole back.

SMALL PEOPLE

The Playdate Secret

'M A BIG FAN of the Cheap Trick: the itty bitty effort that packs an impressive punch. The trifling gesture that draws the sort of "ooh"s and "ahh"s you never have, and never will, deserve.

But I've mastered so few of them. I can't make a three-ingredient crowd-wowing cake, or sweep my hair into a head-turning up-do with the flick of a wrist. I've never even figured out how to rock those cool ribbon embellishments atop a wrapped present.

I have one great trick, though. And to make up for the undue kudos it nets me, I'm going to share it with you.

The next time a friend complains of being overtired, overwhelmed, and over-worked, put your hand on her shoulder and say, "Why don't you drop your kids at my house this afternoon for a playdate, and take a few hours for yourself?"

And say it like you mean it. Like the idea doesn't terrify you. Because here's the crazy thing, the dirty little secret about having other children over to your house: It's actually easier than not having them.

Everyone knows the Law of Progeny Pandemonium, that the chaos within a family home increases exponentially with each child you shlep home from the hospital. But the law doesn't hold if the youngsters bursting through the front door are not your own.

In fact, there's a shocking reversal-of-chaos phenomenon that ensues when your offspring have someone else to play with. Someone else to nettle and tug on and tease. Someone new, who finds those tired old Lincoln Logs "cool!" and the long-forgotten swing set "awesome!"

Sure, they need help reaching toys on high shelves. They demand snacks. They make messes. But the way I see it, any playmate who's potty trained is less trouble for me than enduring another mind-numbing round of Go Fish or folding my unlimber body under the coffee table for Hide and Seek (or as I like to call it, Hurt and Creak).

Even as I'm getting credit for being a generous friend — racking up points as the "fun" mom who relishes the blessed company of all precious children — I get to paint my toenails in solitude or check my email or hole up in my bedroom with a saucy book while the kids are ... while they're ... okay, I have no idea what they're doing out there but that's really the whole point.

"Except for the occasional making of sandwiches, saving the playmate from drowning in the pool, and spinning them on a tire swing, I get tons of work done," agrees a friend of mine who knows the playdate trick. "It's so worth it."

The greatest part of this scheme is that even when your friends get wise to it — when they realize that by dropping off their kids at your place, they're actually doing YOU a favor — you won't be reproached. You'll be rewarded with a reciprocal playdate at their house so that they, too, can appear to be givers while surreptitiously avoiding the dreaded daily "what do we do 'til dinner?" dilemma.

About the only downside to hosting playdates at your home is that it's addictive. My neighbors have discovered the buddy-buffer trick and now we both dispense with any pretense and simply ask to borrow one another's kids. All the time.

"Can I borrow your son for an hour while I try to get some yard work done?" they shout from their lawn.

"Sure," I call back, "if I can I borrow yours tomorrow morning. I need to practice my up-do."

Baby Einstein Refunds

HENEVER I THINK I'm doing a decent job of raising my kids, something happens to convince me that I am, in fact, profoundly inept at the job.

Most recently it was the news that the Baby Einstein company is offering refunds to anyone who bought its DVDs in the last five years. Here's why: Turns out the show doesn't actually make kids any smarter.

I know. It's shocking. Next they'll tell us that Froot Loops are *not* actually part of a nutritious breakfast, and that sparing the rod does *not* in fact spoil the child. Where will the madness end?

The Einstein videos — and the Baby Beethovens, da Vincis, and Wordsworths that make up the whole lofty-tot series — have long been promoted as educational, said to stimulate babies' brains. But a child advocacy group called the claims untrue and threatened Disney with a class-action lawsuit, citing studies that prove such shows actually delay language development.

In other words, the more they see, the less they know. Which is sort of how I feel about my parenting skills.

Confession: I'm one of the lousy moms who strapped her infants into their no-escape high chairs, pushed them in front of the television and popped in a Baby Mozart video. I did it with frequency and I did it with confidence, believing for no good reason that the images of low-budget puppets nodding to sonatas would spark synapses in my boys' burgeoning, Harvard-bound brains.

Because it was either that or my well-worn copy of *The Rocky Horror Picture Show*.

But the truth is I didn't screen Baby Mozart for my kids. I did it for me. For the 30 minutes of divine alone time that those bizarre, baby-bewitching shows provided once (okay, sometimes twice) a day. In a sprawl of groggy home-with-my-infant months, that half hour was time when no one whined at me. Wailed for me. Tugged on me. It was time so precious that I don't even mind having traded a few of my kids' IQ points for it.

Yes, I'm going to take the "La-la-la-I-am-not-listening" approach to this refund news. You can argue that the videos inhibit language acquisition, that children learn to speak through face time with mom and dad. And I can argue that my kids did not need to learn the words that would have been spewing out of my face if I hadn't had that brief daily window of me time.

Researchers are always telling us what babies need: sleep, touch, attention. No one ever asks what mommies need. When my kids were babies, I needed a shower. I needed a nap. Frankly, I needed a drink. Instead, I calmed my nerves in a bath, took a brownie out to the garden, stole some short-term shut-eye, or lost myself in a book that made me laugh — and laugh in a way that a post-diaper-change game of "where's your nose?" really never did.

My kids loved the Baby Einstein series. They'd coo and giggle and stare stupefied at it from the second I hit "play" through the last doleful strains of the closing-credit music. But I can't say whether the content was terrific, since I rarely saw it myself; if it was on, I was elsewhere in the house. For the record, though, I learned phrases in a dozen other languages from hearing the thing in the background, so if it stunted my kids' smarts, at least it bolstered my own. Domo arigato, Einstein-san!

Parenting is hard. And having a little confidence that you're doing the right thing — for example, exposing your baby to something educational while you expose yourself to, say, something chocolate — is an inestimable blessing. Even if it's unjustified.

That's what I think. But then, I'm no Einstein.

Hop on Pop

I'S THE GREAT IRONY of having children: The very act that launches you into parenthood is difficult to achieve — ever again — once your kid is born.

It's like nature looks at you and says, "What? You got what you came for. Find another way to jazz up your evenings."

And it happens to everyone: No matter how much your boudoir tends to bounce before Baby comes along, it slows to a sort of sad, silent stillness (sigh) once the diapers start flying.

"I can't think of a single couple I know who hasn't been affected by this issue," says sex therapist Ian Kerner, a New York husband and father of two.

But he swears there's hope. In his new book, *Love in the Time of Colic: The New Parents' Guide to Getting It On Again*, Kerner and co-author Heidi Raykeil say there's no reason to throw your libido out with the baby's bath water. "It really is possible," they write, "to do the hokey pokey and keep up the hanky panky."

What causes the sexual fizzle between new parents? Exhaustion. Stress. Mom's hormones, and her tendency to devote every amp of energy and inkling of empathy to the helpless, gurgling humanoid in the bassinet, leaving none for poor, pent-up Dad.

Kerner jokes that a working title for his book was "What to Expect When He's Expecting Sex" because Dad's urges — and Mom's reluctance to have her arms, breasts, and hair tugged at by yet another needy family member — are a common source of strife.

I remember those post-baby months so clearly: Sex felt like another chore on my household to-do list, rather than the delicious indulgence it had always been. I was confused, disappointed, and embarrassed at having gone from fit and frisky to tuckered out and turned off.

Kerner says it's just as tough on guys. He confesses to having been so hard up after his kids were born that he once became aroused while listening to his wife read the book *Hop on Pop* to their son.

He's not alone. I recall my husband trying to woo me with *There's a Wocket in My Pocket,* and I think we can all agree that when you're hearing innuendo in Dr. Seuss verse, it's been too long.

Here's good news, though: Kerner says that by expecting sex, a new dad actually is performing a vital task — luring his partner slowly (if sometimes annoyingly) back into a strong, passionate couplehood, "a crucial necessity if they're to flourish and succeed as a family."

Kerner insists there are two ways to do that.

Wrong way: "Just saying, 'Let's have sex now.'"

Right way: "Communicating, building anticipation, helping a woman rediscover those feelings of wanting, helping her to feel sexy, contributing to all the new chores that go along with having a baby in order to help her de-stress."

Pay attention to that last point. Along with all the other surprises of new parenthood, I was shocked (who knew?) to discover there's nothing sexier than a guy who can swaddle, shush, and sway a newborn to sleep. Sorry, that's hot.

As your kids grow, of course, new sexual challenges arise. We recently entered the Kiddus Interruptus phase and I can promise you that nothing quashes the libido like having to explain to your children why Mommy likes sleeping with "just her boots on."

Once you're past the baby years, though, the solutions get simpler. Communication? Anticipation? No need when basic hardware does the trick.

Says Kerner, "We have a lock on our bedroom door."

My Son's Peaceful Defiance

P ARENTS CAN BE so smug. We think we have life's puzzles solved, and that our kids are callow dimwits desperate for our guidance. Admit it: We think of them as dense, doughy biscuits requiring the heat of our unparalleled wisdom to rise to their fluffy full potential.

Lately, though, I've been wondering if we're wrong. If, in fact, our car seat-bound offspring are the ones who have the answers and we grown-ups are too culturally programmed, too set-in-our-ways, to see it.

The notion strikes when I ask my three-year-old to put on his shoes. Or clean up his toys. Or turn off his video, come upstairs and take a bath. That's when he looks at me with utter impunity and says, "I won't."

There's no willfulness in his voice. No shame. No guilt. "I won't."

He's simply stating a fact, letting me know we're going to have a problem here if I insist on pursuing this ridiculous mandate.

There's a look — is it peace? — that crosses his peanut butter-smeared face when he says it, and I'll admit the whole situation stymies me. My linear adult thought process goes like this: How do I get the child clean if he won't get in the tub? How "clean" does a person really need to be? What will his preschool teachers whisper when they notice the same dirt smudge that was on his knee yesterday … and the day before?

But his behavior also kind of inspires me.

Where do you get that kind of moxie? Are you born with it and does it dissipate with age? Is it gradually paved over by parental praise, "good" grades, and society's other rewards for cooperative behavior? And if so … can you get it back?

Because there are lots of times when I'd like to look people smack in the face and tell them dispassionately, "I won't."

The hostess, for instance, who tells me I have to wait 20 minutes for a patio table. Or the Costco cashier who informs me that these coupons aren't valid until tomorrow and I'll have to come back then.

This must be how my son feels when I impose my agenda on his. It's not personal. It's not a plea for autonomy. It's this: The information he's just heard registers as utterly, abominably wrong. It offends his sense of fairness, stings his understanding of how the world should operate.

"Look," his two words tell me. "I kept my shoes off the couch. I ate those ghastly green beans. All I want is to go about my business without you bossing me around for 10 minutes. Is that so much to ask?"

I got an email this week from a company I work for.

"We received your invoice, but you need to fill out these [multiple, maddening, mind-numbing] attached forms and fax them back before we can cut you a check."

What I said: "Sure thing. Thanks." What I wish I'd said: "I won't."

There's the ATM machine that asks if I will accept a $.50 processing fee. The road signs that show my freeway exit is closed and I'll have to take a two-mile detour. The voice in my head insisting I should really skip dessert considering what I ate for lunch.

Hmph. Watch and see if I will.

We grow accustomed to being ordered around. We accept it. We barely even notice it after a time. And we rarely, if ever, speak out in opposition.

I'd like to be humble enough to respect my son's defiant decisions and learn from his fearless approach to life. I'd like to be free-willed enough to look society in the face and occasionally say, with peace on my face, "Ain't gonna happen."

But let's face it.

I won't.

Parents' Wise Words

I'M WHAT THEY CALL a word person, preferring "viridian" to dreary green and never uttering "confused" when "flummoxed" is within reach.

An English major whose motif-musing and allusion-hunting skills have proved all but useless in the real world, I take admittedly odd delight in the careful craft of sentence-smithing.

One of my prized possessions is a tome titled *The Highly Selective Thesaurus for the Extraordinarily Literate*, and I fling myself from bed each morning to savor my Word of the Day email from *dictionary.com* — a wellspring of toothsome terms like numinous, doff and foofaraw.

I challenge myself to use each new word in conversation before the week is over, and just never you mind whether or not I'm successful. The point is I want to.

That is why I find parenting to be a bit of a bore. As a mother, I estimate 87 percent of the sentences that spring from my mouth are vapid. Artless. In fact, they border on asinine. And most of them should go without saying:

"Stop hitting yourself." "Get your jacket out of the peanut butter." "No spitting in Mommy's bed." There's the perennial, "You must use a tissue for that" and the all-too-frequent, "Well, would you like it if I called *you* an oogie bananahead?" I recently heard myself say, "We never ever lick the bottoms of our shoes." And I wondered what the devil had become of my dexterity for discourse — let alone my children's common sense.

I realize that human beings aren't born with an aptitude for basic hygiene and social etiquette, and mine are no exception. Friends tell me they've been shocked to have to articulate these instructions to their offspring: "Stop picking your sister's nose." "Please don't hump your pillow in front of other people." "Do *not* throw the cat in there again."

Others never thought they'd have to say this: "Yes, underwear is a requirement at the dinner table. Particularly when you're not wearing pants." Or this: "If you went pee-pee in the bath water, you probably should not be drinking it." One recently found herself offering this string of seemingly self-evident edicts: "Get your hands out of your pants." "Get your hands out of *her* pants." "Go wash your hands."

I have faith our kids will memorize all of these rules eventually and there will be no need to whisper, "Stop pulling up your shirt" as they walk down the aisle. (If there is, at least we'll be able to employ more graceful language by then, such as: "Darling, do refrain from exposing your thorax. It's entirely inappropriate to both the venue and occasion.")

Meanwhile, though, I confess I'm disappointed with my role as Declarer of the Dull Directive. Deficient in other motherly assets, I always assumed my love of language would compensate for my lack of patience and my distaste for holiday handicraft. Indeed, my favorite parenting moments — the few that leave me feeling especially well-equipped for this job — are when my kids ask me to explain an abstract concept like death or sarcasm or spongecake and I can discharge a chain of images and metaphors that leave them sitting silent, their eyes shifting and unfocused as they process the description, and then lead them to a clear-as-a-windowpane, "Oh!"

So forgive me if spewing phrases like "Don't let the dog lick your privates" feels like wasting the paltry parental proficiency I possess. And not just wasting it, either. Squandering! Nay, fribbling it away like so much worthless foofaraw!

I'm sorry. But it had to be said.

Breast Milk Canapé

I CAN'T HELP it. I see the word "brasserie" and I think "brassiere." It may be Freudian, but a controversial dish at a New York City eatery has — just this once — justified the slip.

Diners at Klee Brasserie in Chelsea recently got a taste of Mommy's Milk Cheese, a delicacy made from (gulp) human breast milk. Chef Daniel Angerer whipped up the fromage-de-la-femme after discovering that his home freezer could no longer hold all the milk his wife was pumping for their 10-week-old daughter.

The couple hoped to donate the extra milk to families in need, but the approval process takes months. So rather than waste the current stock, Angerer, who once defeated Bobby Flay on *Iron Chef*, conducted a culinary experiment. He liked what he tasted, and he soon began experimenting with the cheese at his bistro as a canapé in various incarnations: encrusted with caramelized pumpkin, coated in dried mushroom dust, accompanied by figs and Hungarian pepper.

Some foodies loved the idea; others found it appetite-curdling. Veteran restaurant critic Gael Greene said it wasn't the mild taste but the "strangely soft, bouncy" texture that creeped her out.

Breast milk — technically — should be one of the healthiest things people can put in their bodies. But since the source (Angerer's vegetarian spouse) is unregulated, the health department won't allow it on the menu. Which probably is for the best. My problem with Mommy's Milk Cheese isn't gastronomical. It isn't even Puritanical. It's personal.

New mothers are told unequivocally that providing breast milk is the single best thing we can do for our babies, so we go to preposterous lengths to wring every precious drop of "liquid gold" from our poor, pawed-at bosoms.

We study the "football hold" and "cradle hold" like we're cramming for a chemistry exam. We strap hideous flap-bras onto the food factories that used to be our man-bait. We avoid delicious colic-triggering treats like chocolate, and pop quizzically named herbs that make our sweat smell like maple syrup. And we pump. Oh, my gouda, do we pump.

Anyone who's ever hooked her mammaries to a slurping suction machine can't relish the idea of serving her hard-won créme de la créme with crackers, you know what I'm saying?

Pumping is work. I have friends who've pumped under ponchos at church, sitting on airport floors, and in Starbucks bathrooms with customers knocking to get in.

One gal, a radio host, pumped while she was on the air, wired with a microphone and sitting in a bathroom down the hall from her male co-hosts' sound booth. Corporate moms often pump in shabby storerooms and out in their cars, with beach towels covering the windows.

One friend, a magazine editor, knows too well the rigors of pumping. She left her baby at home to cover Couture Week in Paris (I know, I know, that's not the hard part) and had to carry a hand pump to relieve her hyper-productive ducts between shows. "Imagine rushing in the bathroom at the Chanel showroom to express milk, skipping out of an Hermès luncheon to relieve my swollen breasts in the back stockroom, and dashing out of Dior because my shirt was soaking wet," she says. "The saddest part was having to dump it into the sink every time."

The stuff is invaluable. It's mommy moonshine; every ounce counts, which is why it's hard to watch it rolled into bite-sized haute cuisine.

Angerer reportedly is developing a new recipe for his wife's breast milk: gelato. And while I do consider frozen dessert to be a higher calling than overpriced appetizers, the dish still feels misguided. If the ice cream is chocolate, his nursing wife can't eat it. And if it's not ... then really, what's the point?

Infernal Artwork

T HE WOMEN WHO GUIDE my son through preschool are more evolved human beings than I am. They have unlimited capacity for appreciating his every tiny accomplishment, every endearing utterance, every minor scribbling and random stroke of a glue stick.

They send home stick sculptures and pudding paintings, stencil sketches, and piles of scraps that he spent the morning snipping with safety scissors.

I make the requisite fuss at pick-up: "Wow! Look what you did! You've been busy! What a cool … submarine-dog?" But stumbling to the car, arms full, I begin to panic. Where is all this delightful evidence of self-expression supposed to *go*?

I resent the mountain of masterpieces that amasses on my kitchen counter daily; there, I said it. Since sentimentality breeds clutter, I've tried approaching the problem with pure pragmatism, but it taught me this: The saddest eight words in the English language are "Mommy, why is my drawing in the trash?"

It's true. I'm going to hell. But I won't be alone.

"We have a daughter who is prolific," Northern California mom Kat McDonald told me. "Anything left behind in the car I throw away. I usually have to shred it because our daughter will cull the trash."

Some moms toss the stuff when the kids are on vacation. Jennifer Untermeyer of Colorado does it after they've gone to bed. "I feel a tiny bit guilty," she said, "but it passes after a glass of wine."

Some things are worth saving, of course — worth preserving in a time capsule that your kids can reminisce over when they're grown. But what to keep?

Most parents agree: 3-D projects have to go. Take a picture, if you must, but kick that diorama to the curb and quick, or you'll be buried by Junior's seventh birthday. Anything made of feathers or food must go, too. Let the kids help sort the "keepers" from the recycle-bin-bound.

"It's important that children learn to let go and organize important possessions," said New York City mother-of-three Sara Lise Raff. "Forming emotional attachments to inanimate objects may lead to a guest appearance on Oprah's 'Life as a Hoarder' episode."

When it comes to whittling the heap, moms say time is on our side. Hide artwork in a folder for a month and then go through it with your kids; you'll find the Crayola creation they cherished in October may have lost its appeal by November.

Beware, though. Clever kids can anticipate — and

thwart — the purging session. "My daughter has gotten clever and now writes 'To Dad' on things so I won't throw them away," lamented Californian Marty Guise.

Here are some other composition-coping strategies I picked up from moms around the country:

• Hang a wire across your child's room and clip her new artwork to it for a week. Then save the very best in an accordion folder, under-bed box or binder with plastic sleeves.

• "We covered the entire wall of our boring laundry room with kid art, and it looks great," said Denise Gavilan of Virginia.

• Technology's a lifesaver — and space saver. Take a digital photo of your child holding his art, or have him explain it on video, to give the piece context for years to come.

• Save your favorite art as screen savers or scan and display them on an electronic slide-show photo frame. Have them laminated as placemats or create a coffee-table book of them on Shutterfly. "It makes a great gift for your child," said Nevada mom Carolina Moore, "and it won't track glitter or sequins through your house!"

• Reincarnate the artwork as wrapping paper or scrapbook backgrounds. Or give it away. "I snail-mail my son's grandparents a subscription to his 'Artwork-of-the-Month Club,'" said New York mom Sky Khan. "That way some of these precious pieces find their way onto someone else's fridge."

Pop Goes the Kids' Bop

I T NIGGLES AT ME all day long. It's poking at my poor, feeble cerebrum even as I try to write this column. And if it were something great — if it were Ray Charles or Led Zeppelin or Elvis Costello — I would welcome the distraction.

But it's not. It's an artless song about bowling by a bush-league children's rock group whose name I won't tell you because I want to say quite a few more rude things about them. Like this: They are to music what Pop-Tarts are to breakfast. A queasying excuse for substance.

Someone gave us the band's CD, and I made the mistake of playing it during carpool one morning to keep the little ones happy. Now it's stuck on "random repeat" in my head. (And note that the ability to invade one's brain does not a meritorious ditty make.)

Kids like it because the lyrics, although clumsy, are quite literal. They enjoy the unremarkable singer's Disney-esque vocal stylings as she faux-emotes about pizza, dogs, and gutter balls. They're fond of the kooky, colorful CD cover.

I hate it for all the same reasons. From Mister Rogers to Raffi, from the Wiggles to Barney to those icky spiritual vegetables, the crowded "children's music" genre echoes with too many preachy, soul-less tunes performed by people whose inexplicable grins are eerily audible as they croon.

Wiggle me this: Why can't kids just listen to real music?

It's true that we introduce our kids to reading via children's books, and we initiate them into the cinema with children's movies. But we needn't ease them so gently — so childishly — into the world of music, because music can be appreciated, enjoyed, and even, on some level, "understood" by listeners of any age or maturity.

Our response to music isn't intellectual, it's visceral. And when you flood kids' virgin eardrums with "Toot Toot, Chugga Chugga, Big Red Car," you're really just priming them for dreck.

Not all kids' bands are awful, of course. I can't get behind my grown-up friends who listen to Choo Choo Soul and the Laurie Berkner Band when their kids aren't even around. But I'm fond of Schoolhouse Rock and Trout Fishing in America, both of which — like all good art — affect us in layers.

Music should give us something to delight in right this minute, and keep providing interest each time we hear it — even if the interest on the 43rd listen is just nostalgia for the rhymes, rhythms, harmonies, and metaphors we discovered during the first 42 times.

You want simple melodies and arrangements for your

kids? Try the Beatles, Pete Seeger, or "The Lion Sleeps Tonight." You like bright and happy? Play ABBA, the Beach Boys, Jason Mraz, or the soundtrack for *Hairspray*. For straight-up silly, you can't beat the Talking Heads, Barenaked Ladies, or Prince's "Kiss."

Music is a treasure hunt. Every listen should take you closer to finding that one genre, that band, or even that singular song that synchs up with your psyche and ignites an unnamable joy that starts in your ears and spreads to your head, chest, hips, and toes. It should move you. It should exhilarate you.

And Barney can't do that.

My oldest son wasn't three days old before we discovered — out of sheer desperation — that he would stop crying and become utterly, blissfully lost in Kool & the Gang's "Jungle Boogie." Now, I'm not saying he's a better person because of his early exposure to funk. Or because he prefers, to this day, to hear a growly "Git uppa with the git down!" to a perky "Bowling, bowling with you."

I'm just saying if something has to get stuck in my head …

The All-Nugget Diet

EAR PICKY EATER of Mine,

I love you dearly. But you're going to have to bite me.

I'm done with the dinnertime drama. The passive-aggressive poking at your peas. The pantry full of bland, beige, carb-crammed kidnip that makes up your undigestible diet. Cereal and crackers, chips and tortillas, rice and French fries. What are you, a park pigeon?

The fact that your four-year-old body still has the energy to jump on the trampoline and the cognitive focus to work a jigsaw puzzle is, I'm certain, entirely due to the fact that I manage to get three to five soy beans into you every week by bullying you and bribing you with cookies.

I'm not supposed to do that, you know. I'm not supposed to use dessert as a reward. Or cook you separate meals from what the rest of us are eating. Or allow the family table to become a battleground upon which I demand that you nourish yourself, and you take cruel glee in reminding me that I can't make you.

The experts say I'm doing it all wrong. And by the way you bellow, "that's YUCK!" at the sight of a bell pepper, I can see their point.

It's not all my fault, though. Your brother is an adventurous eater who's been happily swallowing sushi, tofu, and artichoke dip since he could say the word "delicious." How was I to know you'd be so fussy? How could I have predicted your taste range would start off so meager and then — inexplicably, alarmingly — shrink from there?

Remember when you used to like eggs? And yogurt? And hummus? Ew. Ick. No, thanks. Then there was the time you begged me to pay — in advance — for a year's worth of pizza lunches at preschool, then cried every Friday because you had to eat it. You're killing me with this stuff.

But you're crafty. You've got me running all over town hunting down those chicken-ish nuggets shaped like dinosaurs. (Not the ones shaped like Mickey Mouse! Not the other brand of dino nuggets! The ones from crying-out-loud Canada!) It's the only meat you'll touch, so I tell myself that the value of eating something whose primary ingredient is not "enriched wheat flour" outweighs the potential risks of ingesting processed, breaded, frozen mini-pterodactyls containing something called guar gum and, gulp, L-Cysteine Monohydrochloride.

I'm probably wrong.

But the child nutrition experts are wrong, sometimes,

too. They proclaim, "Kids love to dip! Serve them veggies with cups of ranch dressing!" They instruct, "Make mealtime fun! Arrange healthy foods in the shape of a funny face!" You won't have it. Any attempt to cute-up your lunch earns me a look that says, unmistakably, "You could dip that zucchini in hot fudge and roll it in jelly beans. I'm not getting near it."

To be honest, I'm impressed with your resolve. When I hand you a plate and you don't like what's on it, there's never any panic in your voice. No latent fear that I might somehow succeed in getting the morsels down your gullet. There's only chilling certainty. "I won't," you say. And you don't.

But I'm tired of the hassle, frankly. I've had it with nuking your nuggets or toasting your waffles while I'm busy chopping and broiling a healthy, colorful, balanced meal for the rest of us. The experts — and let's give them one more chance, shall we? They don't call them that for nothing — assure me that when you only offer one choice, eventually, after much pouting and tummy-grumbling, it will be eaten.

So you win. We're all switching to nuggets. Guar gum be damned.

Pool Spawn

SWIM LESSONS ARE DAD'S DUTY

P REGNANCY IS A slog. For me, there was 4 p.m. nausea and 2 a.m. charlie horses. There were sore breasts, fat feet, and a humiliating resemblance to the *Fantasia* hippos when I slipped, foolishly, into sexy lingerie.

"Poor you," my compassionate husband often said. "You're going through so much."

Each time, I told him the same thing: "It's okay. You're doing the swim lessons."

Different people dread different points on the parenthood continuum. Some fear labor and delivery. Others cower from potty-training. Others cringe at the notion that someone will eventually hand their graceless offspring a driver's license.

My personal Misery Milestone is the one that has me leaping from a soup-like public pool with a slippery toddler and plodding through cold puddles on slick cement in search of a restroom where I must wrestle with said toddler's rubbery swimsuit and stand dripping and shivering while he uses the toilet, then looks up at me with chlorine-reddened eyes and chatters, "R-r-ready to g-go b-back in?"

Any mom who's been baptized in the church of swim lessons, who's donned her least revealing tankini and descended hesitantly into the wet world of "kickers" and "splashies" and other words one would never say in a board room, knows that swim lessons don't improve as your child ages. They just shift.

Instead of being clawed at by your sinking spawn, you get exuberantly kicked in the gut. Instead of wailing into your ears in horror, they squeal into them with glee (who knew water had such extraordinary properties of amplification?).

I'm not what you'd call a worrier. My kids do flips on the trampoline, skip through parking lots barefoot, and play tackle football, all with my blessing. But when I watch my un-buoyant boys gasp and sputter for breath while a relative stranger barks at them to "kick harder!", I have to fight the urge to leap onto the instructor and beat her severely with the nearest foam noodle. Call it instinct.

Also, I find my enjoyment of wet and my tolerance for cold have eroded over the years. I never thought I'd be the "don't splash me" mom. I was the kid who leaped into our pool before breakfast and had to be dragged out, pruney and green-haired, when the sun set each day. But that was back when "pretty" could be achieved with just wet eyelashes and sun-stung cheeks, back before I needed luminizers and revitalizing mists to look merely "not ill."

And at the risk of being relegated to life's, um, shallow end, let me say this: I resent being dragged weekly into the vexing, eternal wax-or-shave dilemma.

So I've decreed that swim lessons are my husband's duty. Other moms do the same — and find ingenious ways to justify it.

"Unlike soccer or ballet or gymnastics, kids have to learn how to swim. It's life-or-death stuff. It's a survival skill," says a friend of mine with two daughters. "Hence, it falls very clearly in dad's domain. Like changing a tire.

"The fact that handing over the job to dad spares us from having to appear in public in a bathing suit is a pretty nice perk, though."

Oddly, my spouse never complains about having to go. In fact, he almost seems to enjoy it.

"It's only half an hour," he says, with a shrug. "And it's fun to see him make progress each week."

But … the incessant shivering? The deafening squeals? And all that talk of kickers??

When pressed, he confesses the task is made more bearable by the presence of half-naked women — a bonus he calls the "hot mom factor."

Fine. Good. Would someone hand me that foam noodle?

Sex Talk

WHERE'S THE STINKIN' STORK
WHEN YOU NEED HIM?

W E MODERN PARENTS are so enlightened. Unlike our Dark Age ancestors, who whacked through the child-rearing jungles with dull old saws like "curiosity killed the cat" and "children should be seen and not heard," we encourage kids' inquisitiveness.

We quench their thirst for knowledge by reading them books about disgusting insects and having long talks about thunder: "I have no idea where it comes from. Good question, sweetie! Let's look it up!" My son's favorite PBS cartoon always seems to be explaining why mold grows on sandwiches.

Because our generation applauds children's curiosity. We reward it. We even brag about it. Until the day it turns toward our underpants, and then we freak the flip out about it.

That happened to a friend of mine last week. Another parent in her son's preschool brought a newborn baby into the classroom, and the tots began asking her questions.

One piped up with the inevitable, "How did the baby get in you?"

While curiosity may not kill a cat, it can do serious damage to a postpartum female. Caught off guard and loathe to decide for other families when — and, dear god, how — this delicate topic should be broached, the new mom explained that she and her husband had engaged in strategic "hugging."

"Oh!" interjected my friend's son, delighted to contribute to the conversation. "My parents hug a *lot*."

After she stopped laughing, my friend started worrying. Did she need to correct this misunderstanding, lest her son think he's getting a baby sister every time his parents go in for a hi-honey-I'm-home embrace? And if so (gulp), how in the uterus does one explain nooky to a four-year-old?

Don't get me wrong. We 21st-century parents are willing to have "the sex talk"; we just thought it would come … later. And with luck, even later than that. On the one hand, why should someone who can't even distinguish between left and right need to know the complex, life-giving mechanics of human genitalia? And on the other … why does the prospect so unnerve us?

"Personally," said my big-on-hugging friend, "I'm just afraid of freaking him out." It's a legitimate concern. When it comes to birds-and-bees discourse, experts tell us to answer only the specific question our child is asking, and no more. But vague explanations can backfire.

When another friend's six-year-old daughter asked her to define sex, she said, "You know how you like it when I rub your back, and kiss you, and hug you? It's like that — but without your clothes on." Two weeks later, her husband went to read their daughter a bedtime story and came running downstairs hollering, "She just asked me to have sex with her, with my clothes on!"

Realizing she'd left out too much information, the mother sat her daughter down and — take two — offered up the clinical truth.

"That's disgusting," the girl concluded. "You're lying."

To be honest, some of us fret less about squashing our kids' sexual psyches and more about fueling their playground talk. I've been the parent of the little angel who gives anatomically correct biology lessons in the sand box, and let me tell you: No amount of enlightenment can make that phone call feel good.

Mercifully, there's a spate of books that promise to help parents strike just the right tone when talking about sex with their kids. I like the titles *It's Perfectly Normal, What's Going on Down There?*, and my personal favorite, *Some Parts Are Not for Sharing*.

But the best reproductive repartee I've ever heard took place between a woman I know and her five-year-old.

Daughter: Mommy, when I was in your tummy, how did I get there?

Mom: Daddy helped put you there.

Daughter: Did he help get me out?

Mom: Not so much.

The Handoff

FOOTBALL IS MOTHERING INTERCEPTED

MY SON WAS STILL SMALL, and gentle, the first time I saw young kids playing tackle football. We were at a playground. Nearby, a dozen helmeted little boys growled and lunged at one another, looking more menacing than anyone in SpongeBob underpants has a right to. "Hit him! Harder!" ordered the yell-y man entrusted with their care.

I was aghast. What kind of people, I huffed, allow grade-schoolers to whomp and wail on each other like so many cleated hooligans?

And now I'm one of them.

No longer amused by seesaws and swing sets, my son has charged head-first into the grunt-and-pummel ritual of tackle football. I didn't want him to play; I forbade it. But his insistence — and my ill-conceived theory that he would hate it, and we could get this passing fancy over with before his gridiron opponents became bone-crushingly huge — prevailed.

For the last three months, he's been suiting up four times a week to be knocked down and hollered at with 25 other brutes. The endeavor goes against pretty much everything I stand for as a parent.

First of all, it smells. It involves diving into the dirt while wearing white pants. And it encourages boys to do things — like dogpiling — that would elicit a stern, "Hey! What do you think you're doing?" if they happened in our back yard.

Plus, it has sacked our family time. Practice is three nights a week (in the dark, when it's cold, and flu season is upon us, I'm just saying), so we rarely have dinner together anymore.

"We're a family!" the coaches tell the team, and it always makes me "humph." In our family, we value compassion over aggression, empathy rather than intimidation.

But football's playbook is different than parenting's. We advise our kids to be thoughtful and thorough; coaches tell them to "rush" and "scramble." We insist that boys and girls are equals; coaches call them "ladies" when they fail.

If they weren't trying to make mothers nervous, why would they use terms like roughing the kicker, chain gang, shotgun, spike, bomb, and suicide squad? I don't even like it when they run the drill "Meet Me in the Alley"; what kind of behavior is that to be encouraging in minors?!

Our boy plays defensive tackle, which involves hurling himself in front of a highly motivated runner and doing something called "getting pressure up the middle," which sounds painful, or unhygienic at best. There were days during conditioning when he came home so battered and bleary-eyed — hobbling like an old man and clinging to ice packs — that I shed tears. "He's broken!" I sobbed. "He's fine," said my husband, who it's worth pointing out did not gestate the little linebacker.

I'll admit this, though: The kid is fit. He sleeps well. He showers more. And he'll eat any veggie I put on his plate after practice ("Yum, is there any more bok choy?").

I had a scare while watching him play this week. He collided with a wall of players and was slammed to the ground, hitting the dirt harder than made sense for someone barely five feet tall. Then five beefy bodies tripped over and landed on him: Smack. Crack. Thud. Grunt. Oof.

I felt so unfathomably far away from him, unable to help. Frightened and disconnected. One by one, his teammates rolled off him, but he remained still for a split second too long. I felt sick.

"You okay, Roshell?" I heard a boy ask as another reached down a hand and pulled him up. A third patted him on the back. I can't be sure, but from the sidelines it looked a lot like compassion. It looked like empathy.

Guess it's a clean handoff to the Hooligans after all.

Projectile Homework

I T HAPPENS A FEW times a year. My grade-schooler brings home an assignment that promises to mock my poor parenting skills even as it converts my dining room table into a wasteland of Sharpies, index cards, and — often, for some reason — cotton balls.

Historic reports that lay waste to our weekends. Science projects that erupt in family arguments.

"I hate them," says a friend of mine, a mother of three. "They get expensive, take a ton of time on top of regular homework, and, honestly, I don't see my kids learning a whole lot from it."

That's just the problem. I've never understood what exactly these projects are supposed to be teaching: Planning? Research? Handicraft? Super! But I'm a lousy instructor for those things — which is why I send my child to school.

Why can't I just educate him in laundry skills, phone

etiquette, and egg-scrambling 101? And his teachers can school him in finding the cultural contributions of Georgia, diagramming the human heart, and building Egyptian pyramids out of sugar cubes.

I have great respect for parents who enjoy these projects — who clear their calendars, roll up their sleeves, and deftly guide their kids from brainstorming to classroom set-up. But I also admire those who refuse to get involved at all. "We'll wield the spray glue when necessary," says another mother I know. "That's it."

It's us anxious back-and-forthers that make projects so stressful on everyone. "I start off saying, 'You need to do this project,'" says one mom, "but often by the end I feel so invested that I find myself saying, 'Go to bed and I will finish it.'"

"It's a balancing act," explains another mother. "I don't want my kids to feel less than capable of doing the work themselves — and I did already pass first and sixth grades. On the other hand I don't want them to fall on their faces."

But if the finished projects will be displayed before other parents, she says, "then you'd better plan to be involved — because the other parents will be. It's a competition."

It's not the tension between families that gets me. It's the tension within families. I know a mother who lives for class projects, and her oldest son does, too. "He's constantly striving to outdo his last one," she says proudly. "Right now, he's building a full-size catapult." But her younger boy has lower standards, so when the Xbox beckons, he simply declares his projects "good enough" and walks away, she says. "I must breathe very deeply at this point."

What is the value in all this push and pull? (And why, as long as we're asking, has there been a mini Mohawk village atop my clothes dryer for a full year? Are we ever allowed to throw these things away?)

I sought insight from a friend who teaches elementary school.

"The point is the process, not the product," she says. "There's always one where you can tell the kid sat in the garage watching his engineer dad construct it — some parents just totally miss the point."

In order to avoid that mistake, let's all look for the opportunities inherent in our kids' next take-home project. You might see it as a chance to re-learn something you'd forgotten. Or to keep your perfectionism in check. Me, I'm gonna pray the word "shoebox" shows up on the materials list.

It's hard to hate a mandate to buy footwear.

Rated PG for Parental Gaffe

T STARTS LIKE THIS. You're chatting with your kid when a familiar phrase pops into your head. A line of dialogue from a favorite movie of your youth. "Eat my shorts" from *The Breakfast Club*, perhaps, or "Son, you got a panty on your head" from *Raising Arizona*. Maybe you're calling the family to the dinner table, Junior is unresponsive and you find yourself blurting, "Bueller? ... Bueller? ... Bueller? ..."

Then you realize, with a cold blast of horror, that your child has no idea what you're talking about. No frame of reference through which to recognize your superior cinematic literacy.

How can this be? (And this is where the faulty thinking begins.) No offspring of yours is going to go through life without studying the classics, without paying proper deference to the heroes of your adolescence, the big-screen giants whose vast wisdom and extraordinary wit shaped your psyche: Mel Brooks. Eddie Murphy. Long Duk Dong.

So you rent a movie, tell your kid, "You're gonna LOVE this," and plop down on the couch for a family movie night. Which is exactly when the cursing begins. And the full-frontal nudity. And the powder-snorting, pole-dancing, cop-killing and flagrant cracking of jokes so racist they actually make your jaw clench.

People, what the (rated R for language) were you thinking?

I realize the memory fizzles as you age, but I don't recall my favorite flicks containing so much sex, violence, drugs, and blush-inducing skank-talk. In my nostalgia-tinged recollection, *Beverly Hills Cop* was funny. Just funny. It did not end in a chilling, slow-mo bloodbath. In my rosy reminiscence, the word "fish" was the only four-letter-F-word in *A Fish Called Wanda,* and Victoria Tennant absolutely did *not* writhe around on a bed in *All of Me* demanding that Steve Martin call her "a dirty sex poodle." What in the name of Jack Joseph Valenti has happened to these family comedies since I first saw them?

It's not likely these age-inappropriate moments will turn my preteen into a Colt-toting, foul-mouthed, um, sex poodle. In fact, if I didn't remember ever seeing them, maybe he won't either. But they do make for awkward viewing. Remember the ghastly discomfort of watching a movie sex scene with your mother — or your grandfather — in the room? You stare silently, trying not to move, or breathe, hoping the throat-clearing grown-up will forget you're there.

I'm heartsick to report that the feeling only worsens as an adult, because now it's your fault; you're the nimrod who suggested the movie and invited innocent eyeballs to watch.

In this way, movies are different than music. When we listen to Green Day in my car, I know when the swear words are coming, and I can hack up a fake cough or emit a well-timed "So! How about ice cream tonight?" over the offending phrase.

But with movies, you don't remember the nasty stuff until it's upon you. And you're sitting there. Grimacing. Gripping the sofa cushions. Picturing your child holding court on the schoolyard recounting the scene from *Monty Python and the Holy Grail* in which the nuns beg for a good spanking.

Distraction is futile. And so you have a choice to make. Do you leap on the pause button and say, "Whoa! Never mind! Who's up for *Chitty Chitty Bang Bang*?" Or do you quietly let the moment pass without drawing undue attention to it?

Personally, I like to use these as teaching moments and spark a healthy dialogue about what we're watching. "That's a heroin needle," I'll interject. "She's shooting up smack, which is a really, *really* bad idea. Let's see if she dies."

My kid's usually unresponsive, which is fine except that it leaves me with only one decent option.

"Bueller? … Bueller? … Bueller? … "

Little Drummer Boy

F AMILIES ARE NOISY. On any given day, put your ear to the front door of a family home and you'll hear a predictable soundtrack: laughing, whining, stomping, hollering.

But none of these sounds rumble through my house. Rather, they may, but I can't hear them. Because I can't hear anything but this: thwappety thwappety thwappety BAM! BAM! BAM!

My son is a drummer. An enthusiastic one. With beefy forearms and a double bass pedal.

Boogety boogety boogety CRASH! BASH! CRASH!

The kid, I'm just saying, is *loud*.

I remember the ultrasound when we first heard his heartbeat: a soft thub-thub, thub-thub, thub-thub. It was at once startling and reassuring, familiar yet miraculous.

But once he was born, the only thing that would soothe this colicky baby was a rolling groove. Swinging, bouncing, walking. Funk music, disco, reggae.

Then a sadistic relative (you know who you are) gave him a Fisher-Price drum set. Why he took to it, and not his Elmo guitar or toy piano, we may never know. Before long, another sadistic relative (it's a genetic thing) eventually helped him buy a full-scale, take-up-half-the-garage, gleaming chrome drum set.

All those years of soccer teams and sailing camps, karate classes and cotillion lessons — he wasn't especially excited about, or adept at, any of them. But this. This banging. This pounding. This full-bodied, wall-shaking whomping. This he loves.

Thwap thwap thwap thwap SMACK!

Now he's 10, and I don't see how he could have chosen a noisier hobby if he'd taken up chainsaw sculpting. There's nowhere in our house I can go and not be rattled. Upstairs under the covers. Back office with the door closed. In the shower with shampoo in my ears.

His little brother finally had to learn to enjoy *Sesame Street* videos without actually, um, hearing them.

Even with a blanket wadded up in the bass drum and using brushes instead of sticks, his beats jiggle the frames that hold his baby pictures. They pulsate the window panes. They throb in my skull. At least the mothers of pianists, guitarists, and violinists can recognize the songs their little musicians are practicing, and hum along supportively. All I can make out is…well, you know what I can make out: Rocketa rocketa rocketa WHAM!

He's in a band. Because he's cool. So cool that he must wear sunglasses while practicing in the poorly lit garage. He studies drummer fashion, carefully considering the classic mohawks, tutus, and dog collars worn by percussion luminaries like Animal, of the Muppet band Dr. Teeth and the Electric Mayhem.

He tries to convince me that drumming is good exercise. Hmph. "Wipeout" is decent exercise. Anything by Kelly Clarkson is not.

Band practice is at our house since his instrument is positively un-portable. Tween boys show up weekly to make neighbor-appalling noise, consume mass quantites of snacks, and leave empty Gatorade bottles littered on the floor. During breaks, they run screaming through my house or dash lunatic-style through our street before settling back into "Smoke on the Water" or Nirvana's "In Bloom."

Once, one of the bandmembers' mothers brought me flowers. "What's the occasion?" I asked. "Just... because you're the drummer's mother," she said, with a sympathetic smile.

But every so often, when I stop to really listen — perhaps even shake my hips and strum a little air guitar — I'm struck by how good he is. The boy can lay it down. Funky and steady with a great ear, he's a cymbal-cracking master of the same rolling groove that once soothed his poor, suffering soul to sleep.

Now if only it could have that effect on me...

Trophy Atrophy

HEY'RE THE FIRST things you see when you enter my son's room, and the only things he packed when a wildfire neared our home.

They're 10 golden, gleaming trophies, each touting him as a "winner" at T-ball, soccer, basketball. The most recent is a pewter mega-monument he earned playing football — on a team that lost every game by about 30 points.

While certainly a winner in my book, the kid has never once been on a championship team. Or even a mediocre one. Still, he has received more trophies than birthday cakes in his life. And he's not alone.

Mini-athletes get trophies these days just for showing up. They're de rigeur, as much a part of kids' sports now as Gatorade and ghastly, costly team photos. At the end-of-season pizza party (also a given), every team member gets a sizable statuette on an engraved pedestal. Playoff teams probably get bigger ones; ahem, I, wouldn't know.

"Claire got a soccer trophy even though she sat on

her fanny and cried through every practice," says a mom I know.

What's the cost of being so generous with awards that were once reserved for the best of the best? Are we championing mediocrity? Will our kids expect "atta boys" for everything they do?

"There is a definite shift toward an 'everybody wins' attitude in sports these days," says a local dad. "It's good and bad." Getting a trophy was his five-year-old daughter's favorite part of her first soccer season — which explains why, at the start of the next season, she came off the field asking, "Where's my trophy?"

Trophy inflation seems to have started with the self-esteem movement of the 1980s, when pop psychology convinced us that "effort" matters more than "success." Some called this progress; others deemed it hogwash.

"I abhor awarding trophies willy-nilly," says a soccer, basketball, and baseball coach. "I have strong suspicions the trophy industry is behind the 'trophies for everyone' tradition." An outrageous accusation? Perhaps. "I suspect the Trophy-Industrial Complex is behind the subprime debacle, as well."

In real life, loss comes frequently — elections, jobs, relationships — and it forces us to reassess our performance and try harder next time. Isn't it better to let our kids taste disappointment now, when the terms are small, than to "protect" them from it until they're grown?

A friend of mine who works in human resources says that, as young adults, the "participation trophy generation" exudes a distinct sense of entitlement. "We don't give merit raises," she finds herself explaining, "just for doing your job."

But not everyone is anti-trophy. Proponents say the token effigies bolster kids' spirits after a brutal season.

"We aren't rewarding them for not winning," argues one coach. "We're rewarding them for showing up regularly, practicing, working as a team, learning the skills and rules of the game, playing through disappointment and pain."

Well, when you put it like that …

"Kids can be so hard on themselves and feel undeserving even when they played well," adds my cousin, whose children play up to four sports at a time. "Some kids have über-competitive parents and a little trophy may be their only positive reinforcement."

It's a fair point. It's not like we've stopped scoring the games; kids, it turns out, are keenly aware of the difference between bench-warming trophies and VIP trophies. And while they may treasure a thanks-for-playing memento as a souvenir from an exacting season, they'll be the first to tell you this: It's small consolation for failure.

"There are only three trophies I'm really proud of," says a sensible fifth-grader I know, who has won big in soccer, hoops, and music. "The rest I call 'loser trophies' because you get them for losing.

"I actually think they're a waste of metal."

Tweens 'Dating' Tweens

I ALWAYS THOUGHT KIDS HATED to practice. It's an easy assumption to make if you've ever plunked down payments for piano lessons, then had to beg, badger, and bribe your kids to crack the "Teaching Little Fingers" songbook just once a damn week.

I've recently realized, though, there are some things kids love to practice. In fact, they spend much of their childhoods willingly rehearsing for life as a grown-up. They practice parenting by caring for baby dolls. They practice working by donning plastic stethoscopes and lugging toy briefcases around the house.

And when they hit sixth grade, it turns out, they practice dating. My son has informed me that suddenly, and on an almost daily basis, girls are "asking him out."

I try not to snicker, but the semantics alone amuse. Out ... where? It's a funny proposition for a child whose notion of "going out" still means hopping on his bike and cruising the cul-de-sac to spy on neighborhood cats.

"Where, um, do they want you to go?" I inquired the first time he told me.

"I don't know," he replied dubiously. "So I said, 'No, thanks.'"

He has since informed me that "going out" simply means you like someone. "Not regular 'like,' but sixth-grade 'like,'" he explained. "It means, 'I'm attracted to you.'"

Seems reasonable. Heading into adolescence, these kids want to know if they're couple-able, if they're worthy of being a pair, if they like how it feels to be linked to someone outside of their long-standing, tight-knit, same-gender peer group. And, let's face it, they want to see how their social standing shifts as a result of this amorous-ish association.

In our parents' day, they called such coupling "going steady," which sounds more like tightrope walking than sweetheart wooing. Our grandparents' generation called it "going around together," which makes sense for grammar school, since that's really all these kids do.

"Mostly, it just means eating lunch together, maybe talking sporadically," explained a 14-year-old I know who's looooong past such tween nonsense and has a bonafide Facebook-official girlfriend now. "Other than that, it's not really different than what it would be like to be friends."

In typical kid-fashion, though, many want the prestigious "couple" title without having to earn it; they enlist friends — or technology — to help them pop the question. My nephew got asked via text.

"She said, 'U want 2 go out with me?' I typed 'OK,'" he

recounted. They never actually went anywhere, or even held hands, before she broke it off, saying she didn't want a boyfriend — which is easy to understand. All that not-actually-doing-anything can really tax a gal's social life.

I find the dynamics of these little-kid liaisons fascinating. I've learned that "going out" legitimizes what might otherwise be dismissed as a schoolgirl/schoolboy crush. You're razzed for secretly "liking" someone, but respected for "going out" with them.

One mom, whose son is graduating junior high, assures me that the "asking out" process is merely a "sweet, innocent, and probably healthy experience" that's really just "practice for the Big Show in high school."

Before then, though, I'm told that my son will have to learn the rigid protocol of middle-school courtship. "You must hug at certain times, and hold hands at certain times and places," my newly wise friend informed me. "Occasional kisses become expected by the end of eighth grade, I think, and with very few exceptions, 'dating' is limited to group outings to movies."

Her son concurred: "There are strict guidelines — almost like a moral code."

Wait, now. Strict guidelines? Rigid protocol? Personal discipline?! Perhaps there's hope for those piano lessons after all.

Begging for Tuition

I HAVE FRIENDS WHO'VE gone to great lengths to ensure a first-rate education for their kids. Mortgaging themselves silly to buy a house in a better school district. Taking a job at an esteemed private school so their kids could attend for free. Even — and I'd sooner endure AP calculus all over again — pulling them out of sixth grade, midyear, to homeschool.

At least I thought these were great lengths. But a mother in Redmond, Washington, has put them all to shame. Single mom Shelle Curley has taken to begging for cash at a freeway off-ramp to raise tuition money for her son to attend a prestigious dance academy.

Seventeen-year-old DJ was invited to spend his senior year at the audition-only Idyllwild Arts Academy outside of Palm Springs. The boarding school, whose graduates often go on to Juilliard, awarded him a $45,000 scholarship. But his currently unemployed mother had to come up with an additional $7,000 to make it happen.

"All the colleges come there to scout," Curley says. "This is my son's chance at a higher education."

So she held cash raffles and car washes. She sold his bedroom furniture. She scoured CraigsList for items that were being given away, picked them up and sold them at garage sales.

One night, with her job hunt going nowhere and DJ's admission date fast approaching, she burst into tears. Her older daughter joked that she should consider begging at the side of the road.

"I said, 'That's a good idea,'" Curley recalls. "My daughter goes, 'I was kidding!' And I said, 'I'm not. I'm headed out.'"

She inked up a sign: "Single parent. Talented son. Tuition help needed. Just a few bucks till we got it!" She rode the bus to an off-ramp where she had always seen panhandlers and, figuring it must be a lucrative spot, planted herself on the corner.

"I was shaking. I was scared," she says. "I had to remember my kid's face and all the hours of hard work that he put into his classes, the sore backs, the ice on his feet, the Ibuprofen. And I thought, this is a very small thing that I can do for him."

She cleaned up the beer bottles and trash underfoot and "held my head up high." But pride wasn't the only hurdle. One of the corner's regular beggars, a fellow named Toad, ordered her to leave. "He said, 'You're not getting on today. I'm on until 5:30 and then Annie's on till 8:30,'" Curley says. "I told him I have a right to be out here just like you do. So I stood on one side and he stood on the other."

Sometimes she got rained on. Sometimes she got yelled at. "People said I was pathetic, that I was setting a bad example for my son, that he was lazy and how could he let his mother go out there and do that for him?"

DJ didn't actually approve. "It just seemed a little crazy to me," says the teen, who contributed to the savings by weeding for neighbors and teaching cheerleading and dance lessons to local kids. "I don't want her standing out there. She shouldn't have to do that. She's had a knee replacement!"

There were entire days when she made only $8. And there were hours when she made $45. In 10 days, she racked up $300, enough to rent a car and buy gas to drive her son to Idyllwild. I spoke with her on the phone the night they left, and she cried.

"I've had blinders on. I've had a mission and a goal," she says. Once it became clear he could go, it sunk in: "My baby's gonna be gone."

When she returns, alone, she plans to keep looking for work while applying for scholarships, grants, and loans to make up the remaining tuition. (She also set up a website, DJsTuition.com for PayPal donations.) But she's done begging beside Toad.

A lot of parents would make different choices in her situation. A lot of us wouldn't reach for our wallets if we passed her in our cars. I might not. But I admire her resolve. I understand it. As a parent, I've felt it. And I don't judge her. Because the truth is I'd still rather fight Shelle Curley for space on a profitable street corner than homeschool a preteen any day.

Kids and Marijuana

IT'S NOT EASY keeping kids off ganja these days. The world, it seems, has gone to pot. President Obama admits to having "inhaled frequently" in his youth. Hollywood Dudes-of-the-Hour Seth Rogen and James Franco shared a joint (or an authentic-looking prop) onstage at the MTV Movie Awards last summer. Regular moms can get hash prescriptions for anxiety and pick up a dimebag from a clinic on their way to yoga.

Even when photos surfaced this year of Olympic swimmer Michael Phelps taking a bong hit, the nation sort of shrugged with disinterest. Most of his endorsement deals failed to flinch. Last week, Subway launched a new TV commercial featuring Phelps (does he always look that stoned?) and the Sly Stone anthem "Thank You (Falettinme Be Mice Elf Agin)." Can't you just see Subway's board meeting after the bong photo broke? "Fellas! We sell snack food! Tell me again why this is bad news?"

If a guy can suck skunkweed recreationally and still win 14 gold medals, what's to dissuade teens from taking their first curious puff? In my experience, there's only one way to keep your kids from becoming potheads.

You've got to become one yourself. That's right. Light up for the sake of sobriety. Inhale in the name of clean living. Take a hit for the temperance team.

My parents, you see, were big tokers. They smoked dope. They talked dope. They may have even sold dope. In fifth-grade health class, I raised my hand and informed the teacher that THC, the psychoactive ingredient in cannabis, is short for tetrahydrocannabinol. And when I came home from class spouting the potential health risks of smoking it, my parents shouted "Lies!" and stormed the campus the next day to shame my teacher for preaching the ridiculous propaganda of the establishment.

Sigh.

But in fact the school didn't need to convince me not to smoke "Mary Jane," "grass," or "rope," as it was reportedly called "on the street." (Have you ever heard someone refer to reefer as "rope"? I've been listening closely since fifth grade: never.) Getting high was something my parents did; and as such, it was the single lamest thing a human being could do.

I viewed their Sunday-afternoon pastime through the hipper-than-thou lens of youth — and, of course, through a cloud of smoke. Their ritual was predictable, pointless, and passé, the stuff of a has-been generation: Pulling out the stinky wooden stash box. Sliding off the lid. Licking the Zig Zags and rolling up a fatty. Lighting up, sucking too loudly on the soggy end, and talking through clenched throats.

Then their giggles would start. Bursts of baked laughter sent smoke spurting through their nostrils. I never could figure out what was so funny. When friends began proffering spliffs at high school parties, I tried to hide my distaste, but the occasional "Ew! Seriously?" would slip out. Why would I fill my lungs with old-people herb?

I'm not saying I never puffed a blunt. But I didn't do it early, and I didn't do it much. It just didn't hold mystery to me.

Now an "old person" myself, I should probably buy a dub sack (Mom? Can you hook me up?) and take up the habit just to keep my kids on the straight-and-narrow. Then again, with all the inhalants, prescription opiods, and meth being abused out there, perhaps the best we parents can hope for is that our kids do grasp onto good, old-fashioned "rope." At least we'd always know where they were on Sunday afternoons: giggling inappropriately on the sofa.

Or on their way to Subway.

The Family
That Rocks
Together...

THERE'S ANTICIPANT SILENCE as the guitarist plugs in. The whine and screech of feedback. The crisp rapping of two drumsticks as a voice barks, "One! Two! Three! Four! ..."

And the rocking, ladies and gentlemen, has begun.

Only it's not a concert stage or even a smoky nightclub; it's a garage. And it's not a leather-clad band of groupie-dogged rock gods; it's a dude and his dad. Or his cardigan-sporting, axe-shredding mom.

It happens secretly in homes across America — not in silence, mind you, but in seclusion. From the outside, these folks look like normal families, earnestly attempting to fill the age-appropriate roles expected of them: goof-off kid, incommunicative teen, sedate and sober parent.

But inside — perhaps during the unscheduled hour between homework and dinner or on a Sunday afternoon — they're gathering around pianos and bongos, picking up harmonicas and tambourines, pulling out the weathered old Stratocaster, and making music.

Sometimes it's a symphony. Sometimes a cacophony. But the sound, I'm told, is the least important product of the Family Jam.

"It's fun to play with someone who is easily impressed," explained my husband, a longtime guitarist who plays AC/DC with our 10-year-old drummer. "I like being able to pass on what I know about music before he gets too cool to listen to me ... and gets better than me."

The idea of handing off the musical baton to the next generation appeals to Dan Diamond, too — that and the "chance to get my musical rocks off," he said.

Diamond, who learned to play from his dad, now plays blues guitar with his 13-year-old son every week. "If we hear something on the radio we think would be fun to play, we jam on it," he said. "My father died about 10 years ago. I am sorry he's not around to listen and jam with us, but I'm thrilled that [my son] has the ear and skill that I know is inherited."

Laurie Deans took up rock guitar after three years of shuttling her son Avery to music lessons. He's 19 now, and they still "noodle around" when he's home from college.

"It's a great role reversal," Avery said. "It takes you out of the parent-child relationship and puts you in a musician-musician relationship."

Deans and other parents admit there's also a sporting element to learning music with your kids. "Lead guitar is a massively competitive thing — though probably more for guys than middle-aged mothers," she said, "but, yes, I am totally stoked to show off by playing him the 'Stairway to Heaven' solo!"

Their musical tastes differ; she likes heavier rock, and more distortion, than her son does. "But it's great that we've gone through the potentially conflict-ridden teenage years sharing a common interest," she said, "being really passionate about the same thing."

Those of us who don't play (although I do hog the microphone) must assume the joy of the FamJam is similar to that of building, or baking, with your kids. It's the melody of creation paired with the harmony of cooperation.

"There's a certain language to making music," my husband said, "not just chords and notes, but song structure and dynamics. When you play with other people who can listen to what you're doing and respond to it, it's like you can read each other's minds. That's the best part of music-making. If I can teach my kid how to do that, it's something he'll always be able to do, with anybody."

Then there are the, um, other benefits.

"He doesn't care about this yet, but when you hit high school, being in a band is a really good way to get girls interested in you. He'll thank me later."

Rent's Price of Admission

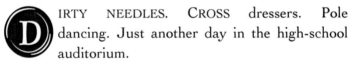

DIRTY NEEDLES. CROSS dressers. Pole dancing. Just another day in the high-school auditorium.

After 12 years of rocking and shocking Broadway, the hit musical *Rent* is exploding onto high-school stages across America. The *New York Times* reports that more than 40 schools plan to stage the rock opera this spring. But some parents and principals are squeamish about the show's racy content, and productions in California, Texas, and West Virginia have been canceled.

The play actually is *Rent: School Edition*, a somewhat milder version of the original. The profanity has been cut — but the provocative plot remains intact.

Winner of a Pulitzer Prize and three Tony Awards, *Rent* is Jonathan Larson's turn-of-the-21st-century take on the classic opera *La Bohème*. It tracks a year in the life of a loose-knit clan of starving artists grappling with poverty, disease, and romance in New York's East Village.

In *La Bohème*, the heroine is a frail seamstress suffering from consumption; in *Rent*, she's a smack-addicted go-go dancer with HIV. If that's not enough to get a parent's trousers in a twist, there are (gasp) gay, bisexual, and transvestite characters.

Like *Hair, Chicago, Ragtime,* and, frankly, most good musical theater, the show captures a zeitgeist while illuminating troubling social issues.

"Oh, they're all racy and suggestive," says my friend Cheri, who teaches musical theater to teens. "*Carousel* with its wife-beating, *King and I* with polygamy. You get into *Grease*, and you're talking about teenage pregnancy."

But there's something about seeing social mores shattered in high-stepping dance numbers that makes them less threatening. Was anyone really scared of the gang members, and their jazz hands, in *Westside Story?*

The truth about *Rent* is that its subject matter — sex, drugs and cultural rebellion — is particularly relevant to high-school students. Sure, you'd hope the cast tended more toward seniors than freshmen (and the fact that the show also is being marketed to middle-schoolers, though unsuccessfully, really does feel inappropriate). Ultimately, though, the show's messages are as sappy as you'd want them to be. Every day should be savored. Art should never be compromised. And irresponsible choices really can have dire consequences — at least until the final ensemble dance number.

"When kids do shows like *Rent*, their eyes light up," Cheri says. "They feel like they're part of something that's contemporary, important, relevant, and cool."

A responsible director helps the students understand the pain and the price of the characters' self-destructive behaviors, she says, which not only makes for better performances, but imparts lasting life lessons to the actors themselves.

San Mateo High School in California used its *Rent* production as an opportunity to bring in guest speakers to educate students about drug use and deadly STDs. Seems to me that, if done correctly, staging *Rent* could open up the kind of invaluable coming-of-age dialogue that you just can't get from mounting another vapid version of *You're a Good Man, Charlie Brown.* (Although I wouldn't mind an updated script wherein Schroeder finally comes out and Lucy does time for impersonating a doctor.)

That being said, there is one terrific reason not to hand high-schoolers the script of a risqué, conscience-challenging play like *Rent.* Or *Sweeney Todd,* or *Spring Awakening,* or even *Thoroughly Modern Millie,* with its —surprise! — white slavery subplot.

But the reason isn't the damage the show could do to our kids. It's the damage our kids could do to the play.

I've seen too many earnest but unworldly teens make an inadvertent mockery of powerful social-issue plays, simply because the material was a good decade of life experience beyond their dramatic grasp.

You can't fake that kind of maturity. You can't teach it. And I'm not fully convinced you can rent it.

What Professors Wish You Knew About Parenting

 TEACH WRITING TO college students. I school them in story structure and tone, coach them in voice and diction.

My students teach me things, too. I've learned, for example, how ridiculous the phrase "Professor Starshine" sounds. I've learned that making literary analogies to *Ghostbusters* — no matter how clever they seem to me — is inscrutable to people born in 1992.

But the most important thing I've learned from my students is this simple fact: When a four-year-old pees on the floor, he ought to clean it up. You're looking at me as though I just made another impenetrable *Ghostbusters* reference, but let me explain.

Parents are working harder than ever to get their kids into college. They start saving when their children are born, help them choose college prep courses as early as middle school, and schlep them to transcript-dazzling extracurricular pursuits throughout high school.

But from where I stand — at the front of a classroom of legal adults who show up at a writing class without a pen — I fret their efforts may be off the mark. In fact, some of my campus colleagues and I agree that while today's parents get an "A" in Getting Their Kids Into College, they get an "F" in Teaching the Entitled Little Buggers What to Do Once They Get There.

To be fair, I have lots of amazing students: alert, organized, motivated. But I have some who don't know the basic things a grown-up should know. Like how to keep a weekly calendar. Or affix a staple to the corner of a four-page essay. (An instructor I know tells her students, "There's an entire store devoted to helping you with your problem. It's called Staples.")

My students can write. And from what I hear, they have mad skills in Japanese, macroeconomics, and human physiology. What's missing from their academic record is Common Courtesy 101 and Introduction to Personal Responsibility.

"I wish parents would teach their kids to respect other people's time," says a professor I know. "I want to say to students, 'No, after you come into class 10 minutes late, take the seat farthest from the door and bang your backpack into other people, it's not my job to catch you up on where we are.'"

Professors' pet peeves are students who cut class and then ask, "Did I miss anything important?" or blow off homework and then ask us to create extra-credit assignments to boost their grades. A student once emailed me to say he couldn't attend class because the surf was up.

Such affronts have made me a crabby teacher — but they've made me a better parent. Terrified of producing young adults who can't replace the ink cartridge in a printer or find a ride to school when (gulp) their car is impounded, I've started expecting more from my own kids.

No longer do I pick up the towel that my sixth-grader leaves in a heap on the bathroom floor; I make him come hang it himself. No more do I grimace, sigh, and reach for the Lysol wipes when my four-year-old "misses" the toilet; I taught him how to manage the clean-up himself.

One frustrated professor tells me she rides her second-grader about remembering her lunchbox every day. "It's the exact same cognitive process as remembering to bring your book to your college class," she says, "and I want her to learn it now."

College isn't the place to learn accountability — and I don't know a single professor who considers it her job to teach it. It's your child's last stop before the cutthroat, unforgiving job market. And if Junior's still whining "I can'ts" and ducking behind "I didn'ts" at that point, well, to paraphrase the Ghostbusters, "This kid is toast."

PARENT, THE VERB

Why Have Kids?

NO, REALLY.

I'M SITTING WITH some great old friends from high school, catching up on the last 20 years of our lives. There was a time when we had everything in common, from favorite teachers to lunchtime hangouts to homework due dates. And it's fun — even comforting — to see how much we're still alike politically, professionally, socially ...

But then talk turns to the way we're most different: my kids and their cats.

Often there's judgment implicit when breeders and nonbreeders get to squawking about offspring. But not us. My pals seem genuinely charmed when I brag about my smarter-than-average spawn (whether they find my kids inspiring or my preening adorable, I can't be sure). And I don't question it when they tell me their cats are awesome, their life is good, and that they aren't convinced procreating would improve it. I believe them.

Except ... there's something about the way they say

that — is there a flicker of doubt on their faces? a subtle rise in intonation? — that makes it seem more like a question than a statement. It feels like they're asking me outright: Starshine, why have kids?

And I'm embarrassed that I don't know quite how to answer. Parenting is not for everyone; some days it's not for me. I love my kids almost as much as I love oxygen, but I don't always love being Mommy.

It's exhausting and frustrating pretty much every day. And if you've ever yelled at a three-year-old for peeing his pants, you know that parenthood teaches you things about yourself that you'd have been delighted to never, ever learn.

"There are things I wish I had been warned about," says a friend of mine who has two daughters. "Entertaining them and dealing with other mothers. No one told me."

Indeed, the pros and cons of parenthood are the same: It demands the best of you.

Caught on the spot, I tell my friends, "My life is richer because I have kids. But it's harder."

Over the next week, though, my kids unwittingly remind me of the reasons parenthood is a worthwhile endeavor.

Have you ever made something — baked an exquisite cake, painted a still life, built a porch — that made you fat-full with pride every time you saw it? Looking at my kids' faces feels like that, times a million. Especially when they're sleeping, because that's when they're not asking me for food or money.

Parenthood intensifies your existence. Joy is wider; pain is deeper. It's like living in 4-D. "It is the most wonderful and horrible thing you can do," explains a single mom whose son recently graduated from college. "But the wonder and joy outweigh the horror."

Kids let you relive a chunk of childhood every day. Every single day! I'm buoyed by the pure, unguarded emotions that alight across their resplendently naïve faces. By watching them come to understand the world, I understand it better myself (apparently I was too resplendently naïve the first time around to fully grasp it all). I've got a front-row seat to the beguiling Theater of Human Development, where I get to see how fear is formed, and humor, and grace. And it floors me.

But the two things I like best about having kids is sharing my shrewd if partially deranged world view with someone who's utterly rapt with interest, and being loved immeasurably, even when I don't deserve it.

I don't know if my old school chums will ever decide to have children, but they're smart to give it careful consideration. For all its perks and drawbacks, parenthood isn't something you can undo.

Which works out fine for me. I'm just not a cat person.

The Dirty Truth

 REEZE! THIS IS the parent police. Drop your Windex and come out with your rubber-gloved hands up.

For years you sponge-happy, spore-hunting moms have shamed the rest of us with your spotless counters and sparkling floors. We don't know how you did it, you fiendish scrub nuts, but your houses — your very children, even — were always cleaner than ours, ever implying (silently, so silently) that our families were destined to be dingy.

But you can put down your Pledge cans, ladies. Game's over. Those of us who define "cleaning" as "aiming a Dustbuster" refuse to feel inferior anymore. Science is on our side, baby. *science*!

Researchers are saying that a little dirt in the home, on the hands, or even — gasp! — in your kids' mouths won't hurt them. In fact, it's good for them. It turns out that ingesting the bacteria, viruses, and even (just go with me on this one) intestinal worms found in everyday dirt actually strengthens children's immune systems, giving them "practice" for more serious germs.

Scientists call this the "hygiene hypothesis." I call it the "hallelujah-I'm-not-a-failure finding." It's already changed my life.

The day the news came out, I was having a minor maternal meltdown: working too hard, sleeping too little, yelling at my kids too much. Chaos was closing in. When I tried to relax and enjoy my home and family, all I could do was gaze around the house in horror at all the things that need scouring and sterilizing, polishing and purifying. How do a boy's fingernails get to be that particular shade of grayish-brown? Why is there mud on the stairs? Who knew you had to clean window screens? (Who even knows how to clean window screens?)

My life was dirty. And not in the way I enjoy.

Then I read about Dr. Joel Weinstock of Tufts Medical Center, who told the *New York Times*, "Children raised in an ultraclean environment are not being exposed to organisms that help them develop appropriate immune regulatory circuits." Studies indicate our collective Dread of Dirt may be why asthma, allergies, Type 1 diabetes, and even multiple sclerosis are on the rise in developed (i.e. neatnik) nations. Dr. Weinstock goes so far as to say that children "should be allowed to ... play in the dirt, and not have to wash their hands when they come in to eat."

Which is surprising. What's even more surprising is how relieved I felt upon hearing this news — like a hot, humming vacuum bag collapsing when the appliance is shut off (I'm assuming here, as I don't know from vacuums). I didn't realize how guilty I had felt for the smudges, streaks, and spots upon our lives — and for my unwillingness to tackle them.

But no more. Let the three-year-old drop his peanut butter toast on the floor, sticky-side-down, and then proceed to eat it. Let the 10-year-old run out the door with a clump of dog hair stuck to the Velcro of his lunchbox. Let there be a streak of unidentifiable gick at the bottom of my coffee mug.

Big whoop. Bring it on. You'll notice we have no allergies.

These days, when I visit the home of a Swiffer-clenching, Lysol-huffing friend, I just remember my dirty little secret: When I choose to ignore the occasional sand in the bathtub, when I pretend not to notice the smudged fingerprints on my fridge door, I am ensuring my children's robust health.

And as soon as they discover that watching loads of TV makes kids smarter, well, look out. You supermoms will be eating my dust.

Fathering
Females

W HEN I WAS BORN, the doctor misspoke. "It's a bo... ," he told my parents, "a girl!" I work hard to avoid pondering what it is the guy thought he saw. My dad was surprised to feel a twinge of disappointment. "It only lasted a split second," he assures me. "And I probably wouldn't have felt it at all except for Dr. Slip."

I don't begrudge him his momentary grudge. As the mother of boys, I know that being a yin and begetting a yang can make a parent uneasy. My boys like to beat on things, jump off stuff, and generally behave in confounding ways. And when I shepherd my three-year-old to the bathroom at 2 a.m., I'm ill-skilled to help him aim. Or shake. You might as well ask me to repair a blown head gasket.

Thus do I feel a certain kinship to the fathers of daughters. Girls are complicated, and raising them is tricky — especially when your model for "father" is the fella who taught you to throw a long bomb and "take it like a man."

I know a guy who cursed when he found out his wife was pregnant with a girl. "I remember distinctly yelling '#%!' in the muffled cone of silence my car offered," he said. "At the time, it was just one more thing that I felt was not going my way. I would come to the realization years later that it's your child's personality you fall in love with, and it's irrelevant what that personality is attached to."

Still, dads and daughters occasionally make for awkward pairs. One friend said his little girl was forever scarred when he took her, at age three, into a public men's restroom at Thanksgiving and "there stood Santa, pulling up his drawers in front of a urinal."

Another lamented his artlessness with a hairbrush. "I've stumbled through numerous French braids," he admitted. "The French came up with a braid no father can contend with. I'm still trying to master the simple bun."

"I felt pretty low reading the *My Little Pony* books with its overly sweet names," added another. "I still may burn that book with some speed metal blaring in the background."

One father is considering buying an RV to use as a male safe house when his three daughters start menstruating on synched-up cycles.

Another carefully monitors his household's "sentence velocity," the number of sentences uttered per minute. "It increases with the number of females present," he said. "I've learned that when it gets to a certain rate, it's a good time to empty the dishwasher or catch up on the *New Yorker*. Staying out of the fray gives the impression that I am a 'good listener,' when, in fact, I simply don't comprehend."

There are advantages to being the lone dude in a house chock-full of chicks. "I'm the one who can smush the spider and fix the plumbing," said a father of two girls. "They love me differently. I'm their hero! What beats that?"

He said it's made him a better communicator, too. "My girls ask questions about things no little boy has ever talked about. Grown men don't even talk about them. I'm forced to articulate my feelings to my girls."

My dad said the best thing about daughters is you get to keep smooching them long after the age when fathers tend to stop kissing their sons. "That's a sweet deal," he said.

These dads hope to teach their girls what a "good man" is — and to be educated from them, in turn. "I think I've learned the same things I would have learned with boys," said a father of two young daughters: "The joy of being a parent, how great it is to have kids in my life, and how good I look dressed in a pink tutu."

Sitters:
The Last Stand

OUR FIRST GREAT babysitter in years — the kind who's like family, only smarter — announced she was moving across the country, thereby annihilating our beloved Date Night.

While grim, the news wasn't really surprising. I have lousy luck with sitters.

There was Poor Judgment Girl, who decided to "rescue" our "lonely" dog from our backyard one day while we were gone and bring him to a 100-decibel kegger at her apartment. When we went to fetch him, she was too drunk to come to the door.

Then there was Blatant Liar Guy. We said he and the kids could build Legos, make sundaes, play *Star Wars* Monopoly — anything as long as the TV stayed off. We left; he plopped the boys in front of the tube and told them not to rat him out. They did.

Let's not forget Hormonally Tormented Gal, who said she was taking my toddler to the zoo. Turns out they were at her boyfriend's house, where my son watched *Bob the Builder* while the couple, um, coupled in the next room. Ick! Aack!

And I never did forgive poor Multi-Tasking Lady, who did her laundry at our house and left her lacy thong underwear in our dryer. When I found it, plagued by postpartum paranoia, I accused my husband of having an affair with the sitter. "Yeah," he said, laughing louder than I appreciated, "we had wild sex and then … oh, baby … we did laundry!"

So I'm tired of being polite. I've had it with conducting "proper" interviews with potential sitters. I'm going to tell you what I really want in a babysitter — what I think most parents want — and see if it gets me any closer to sitter bliss.

One: We want you to have your own car. When we say it's no problem to pick you up or drive you home, we're lying. Frankly, if we wanted to spend one more minute attending to someone else's needs, we wouldn't need a sitter in the first place.

Two: We want you to know CPR. We don't know it ourselves, have never met anyone who needed it, and our kids stopped gobbling up "choking hazards" years ago. Still, we like it. In our skewed logic, anyone who can re-animate a stopped heart should have no trouble getting a first-grader to eat his peas and brush his teeth.

Three: You seem to believe that calling our cell phones while we're out is the worst thing a sitter can do. Au contraire. The worst thing you can do is be so afraid to call us that, when our infant won't stop crying, you knock on the neighbors' door and ask them what to do. (Yes, of course this happened to me.)

Four: If we're gone three hours and eight minutes, don't expect us to pay you for four hours. We don't charge you for all the soda you suck down; don't charge us for a couple of sluggish red lights.

Five: Be aware that we check your MySpace page for inappropriate photos. Not because we fear you'll re-enact that nude beer-bong moment in our playroom. But because we know that someone who makes such short-sighted choices might not think to remove a preschooler's "rubber band necklace" before he goes to sleep.

Six: Finally, we want you to be comfortable in our home. So comfortable, in fact, that you don't notice the pet hair clumped under the high-chair, or the sand in our children's sheets. Failing that, we want you to pretend that you don't see it and never speak of it aloud.

I've noticed my own sitters are more inclined to contribute to the household mess than to gag from it.

Guess I'm just lucky that way.

I Ain't No Super Model

VERY SUMMER THE KIDS go spend a week at Grandpa's. It's good for them: They learn to fish and appreciate Abbott and Costello. It's good for Grandpa, too: He gets someone to share his mud pie and mow his lawn.

But mostly, it's good for my husband and me. We take full advantage of our offspring's absence by vowing to pursue distinctly adult pleasures, avoiding Go-GURT and playground sand at all costs.

We go out at night and stay out later than we need to — later than we even want to — just to wallow in the freaky freedom of not having to check in with a sitter. Or we stay home, eat Brie for dinner, and watch R-rated movies at full volume, ecstatic in the certainty that no one will stumble in saying, "Mommy, that prison rape scene woke me up…" We plan marathon sessions of wild monkey sex but never get around to them because, frankly, our mojo has so long been attuned to the family schedule that without the threat of being walked in on, the deed loses some urgency.

But it's okay. Because by about the third day, we realize — with appropriate shame — that what we want most is not to savor the privileges of adulthood; it's to behave like infants.

You see, when our kids are around, we are role models. Reluctant role models, even poor role models, but role models just the same. Under the omnipresent, hyper-vigilant gaze of our still-pliant children, we strive to be exemplary human beings: discreet, prudent, diplomatic, and other terrible, unnatural things.

We don't even realize we're doing it; we're simply in the habit of returning the grocery cart to its rightful spot, ignoring the cell phone when it rings in the car, eschewing a second helping of dessert…

Then suddenly we realize no one's watching us — that we needn't, for the moment, be paragons of personhood. The relief! It's like squeezing into a skin-tight dress and sucking in your stomach throughout a looooooong soirée and then finally, rapturously, letting it all hang out when the party's over.

Only, at our house, the party's just getting started. My husband and I begin leaving clothes on the floor and dishes on the table. We devour cupcakes for breakfast and gargle beer with lunch. We cuss — at the dogs, the poor telemarketer, and the nicely dressed religious solicitors at the door. We squander sunny days sprawling sloth-like on the sofa, denouncing exercise of any sort, and having conversations like this: "Remember pot?" "Yep." "Where would we even get it anymore if we wanted it?" "I think your mom knows a guy…"

It's funny. When our kids are babies, we welcome their curious stares and encourage their careful listening. Watching us put on jackets and hearing us order pizza is the way they learn how the world works. But as they age, the things they discern from observing us are much more personal, more nuanced — and considerably harder to master: how we approach our work, how we cope with frustration, how we talk about friends when they're not listening.

I always thought I could be a good parent if I just stayed focused on my kids; I didn't realize how much of the family's focus would reflect back on me. Imperfect, unpolished, prone-to-cupcakes-for-breakfast me.

Having time to let our feckless flag fly is a blessing to my spouse and me. And by the time the kids return, we're ready to resume role-model protocol and relinquish our sty-making, curse-spewing, flab-inducing ways. But we can't help but wonder: Is that how Grandpa behaves the whole rest of the year?

Enough Love for Two

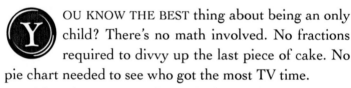OU KNOW THE BEST thing about being an only child? There's no math involved. No fractions required to divvy up the last piece of cake. No pie chart needed to see who got the most TV time.

Sibling-free, I got it all. All the love. All the attention. I got praise for the academic subjects I mastered, like French, and even those I didn't, like trig. When there's no competition, you get kudos for succeeding at arithmetic as simple as this: Love divided by one is one.

It wasn't until I was an adult — and pregnant — that it first occurred to me that love might have a numerator and denominator. My husband and I worried how our beloved dog would cope with having a cooing, pink love-hog in the house. Isn't it a crime to lavish affection on something and then ask it to share that affection with someone new? I asked our vet.

"Love grows," he said.

"What does that mean?" I asked with a seriousness that

should be reserved for conversations about heartworm and distemper.

"The heart expands," he purred cryptically. He was one of those hippie earth-father vets with tons of his own kids and a fluffy, wisdom-indicating beard. "Love multiplies."

Damn it! There would be math.

The dog did get less attention from us; of course she did. But she drew new regard from the baby, who became a toddler, who became a boy, who loved her more than anyone else ever had. Or ever will.

When I became pregnant again, I fretted anew. Wildly in love with my firstborn, I couldn't fathom how I'd find room in my heart for another child. I literally wept with worry. I asked a friend with two daughters how it was supposed to, you know, work.

"You love them equally," she said, "but differently."

It sounded like nonsense to me. Utter gibberish. About as practically useful as the Pythagorean Theorem.

But I've discovered since then that she was right. I don't know if my kids will ever ask me aloud which one I love most. (Do siblings actually do this? The horror!) There was a time when I would have told them that whoever asks that question is the one I love least.

I have a different answer now. One that's better because it's true. There's not a measuring instrument known to science that could detect even the slightest imbalance in the amount of heart-swelling adoration I feel for each of my boys. But I do love them for different reasons, in different ways. I do love them differently.

There are distinct kinds of love. Allegiance. Admiration.

Appreciation. We treasure our mothers differently than we treasure our spouses; why wouldn't we cherish our children in unique ways, too?

I love one of my sons for being such a great role model, and the other for being such a quick study. I love my first child for teaching me to be a mother, and my second for showing me that, well, motherhood isn't something you ever really master.

I love my oldest for demonstrating the cool stuff that happens when you mix my DNA and my husband's in the biological blender; I love the youngest for proving that said blender also has snazzy settings for chop, whip, and liquefy.

I adore my boys for educating me in the basic principle of motherly math — that while our devotion may be immeasurable, it's not incalculable. It turns out that parenting a pair isn't love divided by two. It's love squared. It's an equation so simple that even I can understand it.

But dear god don't give me three.

Sin City

OOPS

I T LOOKED SO MUCH nicer in my head. The way I pictured it, we were going to spend a few days of bond-bolstering family togetherness at a Las Vegas resort that would cater to our every fickle whim. By day we would lounge poolside; by night we'd venture out to ooh and ahh over the city's convenient cultural lessons: the Venetian's canals, Luxor's Sphinx, Caesar's Trevi Fountain.

In my imagination — over-enterprising as it may be — we were going to find freedom in the clean light of the warm desert sun.

Instead, we got drenched in debauchery.

On reflection, yes: It was witless to seek a virtuous vacay in Sin City, the nation's unapologetic adult playground. In the 1990s, Vegas's tourism office made a marketing push to lure families there. But the campaign went bust and the tourism office did an about-face, adopting the decidedly grown-up (notice I didn't say "mature") motto, "What happens in Vegas stays in Vegas."

They no longer woo kids. In fact, the Bellagio hotel doesn't even allow children inside unless they're registered guests, and the new Encore and Wynn hotels have "no strollers" signs on their doors.

But we were heading back from a trip to the Grand Canyon, and the Vegas Strip seemed a natural stop — another mystifying spectacle, not unlike the canyon itself in its dazzling scope and strangeness. Besides, where else can you see Egypt, Paris, and Manhattan in a single road trip?

Getting to those theme hotels is tricky, though. You walk a lot in Vegas, even to catch a cab or hop on the monorail. And strollers are a burden on the city's endless maze of escalators.

You can't get anywhere on the Strip, either, without plodding through casino after casino, and despite the colorful, dinging, video-game-like appeal of the ubiquitous slot machines, kids aren't allowed to play. If they even stop walking long enough to watch Dad play a game, a security guard nudges them toward the door.

Having grown up in our new smoke-free world, my kids were irritated by the cigarette smell in the hotels — and surprised to see people knocking back cocktails before noon.

"Jeez," my 10-year-old snorted, "do people just come here to smoke, drink, and gamble?!"

No, of course not. There's also the hope of some really tawdry sex. Which he found out about during an early evening foray down the city's sidewalks. Gentlemen greet you wearing bright yellow shirts that read "Girls Direct to You in 20 Minutes" and handing out trading cards with photos of naked ladies on them. They don't give them to kids, but a fierce, dry wind blew the cards all over the street. It literally was raining porn, and every time we waited at a crosswalk, my son got a good gander at the gals staring smuttily up at us from underfoot.

Thankfully, the sex business is an equal opportunity offender. The billboards outside our hotel window featured a crush of Chippendale-style beefcakes flashing bedroom eyes and weight-room pecs, and another ad that inspired this question: "Mom, what is a gay escort?"

Kids adapt so quickly, though. We hadn't been there 24 hours before my oldest was encouraging me to climb out of the kiddie pool and enter a dance contest in which I would vie for hoots and cat-calls from fellow sun-worshippers by shaking my bikini-clad moneymaker to a blaring bump-and-grind ditty.

"Pleeeeeeease, Mom?" he begged. "I can seriously imagine you winning!"

But I declined. These things, I've come to learn, tend to look better in your head.

Off-Leash Kids

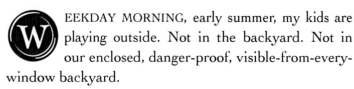 EEKDAY MORNING, early summer, my kids are playing outside. Not in the backyard. Not in our enclosed, danger-proof, visible-from-every-window backyard.

They're cavorting out front. Where there are driveways, blind corners, and a teenaged neighbor with a Pontiac and a lead foot. Where there may be oleander. Or vicious dogs. Or a gun-toting, candy-dangling, meth-addled pedophile.

Maybe not. But from where I sit at this computer, I can't see my kids. And though it makes me sound deranged, I admit this simple scenario puts me on edge. It fans a smoldering lump of fear deep in my gut. As they explore the world beyond our porch, their voices grow fainter, and the voice in my head grows louder: "Lady, you ain't doing your job."

Am I insane? Yes. Also no.

Journalist Lenore Skenazy says such parental paranoia

is the common and natural result of sensationalistic media reports on ghastly kidnappings, gruesome murders, and freak accidents — all of which make society seem far more dangerous than it actually is. Her book *Free-Range Kids* argues that Americans have become so unnecessarily fearful for our children's safety (kneepads for crawling babies? helmets for wobbly toddlers?) that we suck all the joy out of both parenthood and childhood.

Last week, a German boy was hit, and scarred, by a meteorite falling from space. "Do we all go around in meteor shields now?" she asked during a phone interview. "Or do we assume that's a one-in-a-million chance, which it is?"

Skenazy, a Manhattan mother of two, was both cheered and chided on the TV talk show circuit last year after letting her then nine-year-old son ride the subway alone. Raised in Chicago's suburbs, she walked to school starting in first grade. Through an alley, no less. "And it wasn't considered a daring adventure," she said. "It was considered 'The way you got to school.'"

Some hazards are worth worrying about: choking, drowning, lead poisoning, SIDS. But most of our safety fears are irrational. According to the Department of Justice, today's crime rate is as low as it was in 1970, when most of us with kids were kids — and had more freedoms than our children do today. And consider this: Car wrecks are still the number-one kid killer.

"Your child is 40 times more likely to die in a car accident than to be snatched and killed by a stranger," Skenazy said. "And yet we don't shake, shiver, worry, and pray every time we put our children in a seatbelt, because we recognize that's a little paranoid."

Paranoia, she said, deprives our kids of the self-esteem that comes from life's "I did it myself" moments. Do we want to be the people in their lives who tell them, "You're utterly incapable," or do we want to be the ones who say, "I know you can do it"?

Raising free-range kids, Skenazy said, is not about sending them out into the world and hoping they make it back. It's about giving them the tools to be safe, and then trusting them to use them. A little fear is normal, she said. "My kids have heard me lecture 1,000 times on everything from strangers to condoms. And if you knew what a fanatic I am about crossing the street …!"

But planning for every tragic "what if" is not the defining characteristic of a good parent, Skenazy insisted. "Sometimes terrible things happen. I hate thinking about it and it always makes me sound cavalier, but what if your child was in a car accident and it was your fault? Of course you'd be devastated!" she said. "But, would you have been stupid for putting him in a car?"

Family Travels

MORE 'OBLICATION' THAN VACATION

YOU'VE GOT A lot of nerve calling this a vacation. I'm chasing sun-punchy children around a murky pool with a spray can of SPF, wondering how the oldest will survive on his all-Doritos-and-no-sleep diet and why the youngest appears to be missing a shoe. Just one shoe, not both.

I took off work for this. I got a dog-sitter. I'm spending a night just to park my car — the same car that's strewn with minuscule pegs from the inexplicably explosive Travel Battleship game.

This is not hell. I understand: It's family travel. It's togetherness-away-from-home. It's bonding-over-adventures and, more often, *under* adventures.

But it ain't my idea of a vacation.

Where's the cabana boy I was promised? Where's the bottomless blended cocktail and crisply pressed sheets? Where's the blessed silence? The divine stillness? The hallowed, hard-won sloth, for flip-flop's sake?

Vacations used to be different for my husband and me: isolation, rejuvenation, coconut libations. Our idea of bliss is sitting somewhere sunny, doing less than nothing, and consuming our weight (pre-vacation weight, to be clear) in guacamole.

Traveling with kids is more "oblication" than vacation; in fact, it's more work than staying at home. Destinations are limited to those with crank-machines that stamp logos onto copper pennies, and I don't care what kind of yoga practice you rock back home, getting there is a stressful slog. Small stomachs, miniature bladders, and itty-bitty attention spans require frequent snack breaks, bathroom stops, and card games, respectively.

And at the end of it all — though I'm ready to collapse onto anything resembling a pillow, including the duffel bag or even the cushiony shoulder of the zaftig woman squished up next to me in the elevator — my children must be guided to sleep. Read to. Sung to. Coaxed.

I do enjoy spending time with my kids, showing them new things, watching them cavort and, ahem, relax the way I used to. I want them to see the world, and I even want to be the one to show it to them. But it thoroughly drains me.

While some parents seem able to accept that and move on — patiently putting "real vacations" in the "we'll have time for those again someday" category along with, say, gardening and exercise — I'm having a hard time adjusting. I just can't pack a suitcase and put a hold on my mail without feeling entitled to some down time. Some chill time. Some not-upending-a-foldout-bed-looking-for-a-size-two-shoe time.

When I travel with my kids, I go from being Laundry Serf to being Laundry-Serf-Who-Can't-Find-the-Detergent-in-This-Damn-Rental-Condo. I spend all my time trying to find a safe place in the shower for my razor and reminding the boys that the walls are thin, the balcony is high, and that vase is for decoration, not for storing wet bathing suits. (Also, turns out that when a shoe is lost on vacation, it's really lost; you know what I mean?)

I'll say one thing about family trips: My children have a hoot-and-a-half. And why shouldn't they? They've got maid service (me), room service (guess who), and a concierge (hi, have we met?) who can get them reservations at the finest overpriced theme restaurants with the resigned flash of a long-since-maxed-out AmEx card.

I wonder if my boys would enjoy our trips so much if the shoe were on the other foot. But, of course, it isn't. Maybe it's in the vase.

Insanity by Baby Book

SHHH. LISTEN … THERE! Did you hear that? That snarky mumbling? They're doing it again. Taunting me. Shaming me. Making judgmental "tsk, tsk" sounds in my direction.

Yes, I know they're only books. Just glossy hardcover journals. Just pretty pastel diaries with a soft-focus cover photo of some baby's delicious feet. The books look so tidy and innocuous, with their sweet ribbon embellishments.

But we know better, don't we?

We moms know that baby books — those keepsake compendiums where we're supposed to inventory our kids' cute sayings and developmental milestones for posterity — do not exist to bring joy to families. They exist to bring revenue to the gift industry. And to drive me self-loathingly, inferiority-complexedly deranged. (Ooh, there's a nice line for the baby book. Lemme jot that one down.)

Sure, there was a time — when my babies napped often and I was too exhausted to stand up and go make a sandwich — when I wrote diligently, dutifully in those pretty books. "Why we chose your name …", "Our first days together …", "Your first smile …".

But then a full year went by without opening the books again, and I felt remiss. How would I ever remember the name of the song that played on that music box as I rocked them to sleep? How would I recall the adorable way they said "Gumpus" instead of "Grandpa"? And how could I just let those cherished memories fade?

I moved the books to my bedside, where I could scribble in them before bed. Could … but didn't. Another year passed. Oy, the guilt. I moved them to the kitchen counter, where I proceeded to ignore them for another year. Now I vacillate between feeling sick with remorse, and thinking, "You know, those boys are old enough now. If they want to remember this stuff, they can start their own damn diaries."

The worst part is I have no excuse. Sure, I'm busy, but I find time to browse online shoe stores for boots I can't afford; surely I could find time to document the names of my children's first best friends, and the color of the cupcakes at their third birthday parties.

But I came up with some excuses I'm rather pleased with:

1. Like photo albums (anyone remember those?), these books call for only happy memories of good times. The prompts never ask, "How I felt about my episiotomy …" or "The first time you bit me on purpose …" and the journalist in me is uncomfortable with the inherent bias in such lopsided reporting.

2. When my kids became conscious of the books, and started trying to make quips clever enough to earn book space ("That was pretty great, right? Are you gonna put it in the book? No? Okay, listen to *this* one …"), it lost some magic.

3. We don't recognize the precious while it's happening. Have you ever been at a restaurant and noticed the cutest, happiest toddler in the world sitting at the next table — and his mom looks suicidal? That's because we're cruelly blind to cuteness while we're sitting right beside it. And wiping its perennially oozing nose. And asking it to stop crumbling the complimentary Saltines into our purse.

4. The truth is I don't want to rush to the book every time my boys stun, amuse or enchant me, which is daily. Because writing it down means admitting that this fascinating, entertaining chunk of our lives is only temporary. It means coming to grips with the fact that our current reality will ultimately exist only in ink, and nowhere else. And that makes me sad.

5. I can't even hear what's going on in my family's life because of the accusatory racket those books are making in the kitchen. If they would just *shut up*, I'd be the perfect mother. I swear.

Since When Does 'Adult' Mean Dirty?

ROWING UP IS no rare achievement, but we did work hard to get here. Stumbling around the house in our parents' shoes, calculating our ages in cheeky increments of halves and quarters, scrutinizing that slow-growing height chart etched onto our bedroom doorframes in ballpoint pen.

In fact, you could argue that our entire childhoods were devoted to prepping and plotting for adulthood. In my own eager little mind, being "big" meant freedom. It meant confidence. It meant respect.

Imagine my shock to discover that adulthood actually means shopping for vibrating underpants and schmoozing the stars of *Busty Cops* and *Naked Heroines Bound for Trouble!*

Every year, porn stars and erotic toy peddlers gather at the Los Angeles Convention Center for the naughtyfest known as Adultcon. Open to the public, the expo invites guests to meet "over 69 adult entertainers," purchase "male sexual enhancement products" and learn about "vaginal rejuvenation centers."

All of which sound diverting indeed. Stimulating? Maybe. Amusing? Undoubtedly. But ... adult?

Let's ignore the fact that the girls in Adultcon ads appear to challenge even the legal definition of "adult." And let's disregard my own clearly twisted associations of "adult sex" with responsible considerations like love, birth control and (yawn, I know) STD-prevention.

Putting all that aside, you still have to wonder about the pretense — the feigned delicacy — in the event's name. Why can't they just call it Raunch-Con and be done with it? It's absurd for an industry whose money shot leaves zilch to the imagination to suddenly, um, beat around the bush.

Of course, porn isn't the only industry to co-opt the word. Anyone care for an adult beverage? Wanna catch an R-rated movie with a juvenile plot and "adult language"? Adult is now a euphemism for smut, booze and profanity — and while I'm actually fond of all three, I'd rather they didn't define the very developmental stage at which I'll spend most of my life. It's just too sad. This is what we rushed to grow up for? The reward at the end of youth's tribulations is ... an invitation to be crocked, crude and first in line to get Ron Jeremy's autograph?

Call me naïve but I was hoping for more.

I admit that adulthood isn't everything I thought it would be. Turns out confidence isn't automatic when you come of age. I was way off on that whole "freedom" thing. And while I no longer yearn to sprout taller, I spend too much time hoping I won't sprout wider.

But being a grown-up is satisfying in other, unexpected

ways: I like contributing to society in my own old-enough-to-have-some-heft way. And I like having enough life experience to appreciate smart humor, and complex issues, and thoughtful discussions.

Which is what adult entertainment really ought to be, right? Smart, complex, thoughtful. It should be the kind of stuff — Bill Maher monologues and Merchant Ivory films, say — that makes kids shuffle out of the room bored and confused, rather than run screaming, "Eww! What *was* that? Make it stop!"

Thankfully, there are still a few bastions of modern life where "adult" means nothing more than, "Honestly? Your kids won't find this interesting." But it's getting harder and harder for us to recognize them when we see them. A librarian I know says customers get embarrassed and defensive when a catalog search identifies their request as "adult fiction" until she explains that it merely distinguishes the tome from young-adult novels or, you know, pop-up books.

And another friend had a brief moment of panic when I brought up the subject recently. "What about Adult Education?" he said. "I'd better go double check the class I signed up for ..."

Just Say 'Know' to Teen Sex

ROWN-UPS SPEND A lot of time worrying that the next generation is sexually stupid. "Today's teens," the cries begin, and they end with the words "wild," "in such a hurry," or "setting themselves up for heartache ..."

They're not unfounded, these accusations. But they were true of us, too. And they were true of our mothers, grandmothers, and — sorry for the mental image — great-grandmothers. Sex is like driving. Before you slide into the driver's seat and take your foot off that brake, you don't really know anything useful about it. And the education can be terrifying.

My friends learned the hard way. "I didn't anticipate how emotionally overwhelming the experience would be," said one.

"I wish I'd been better educated about STDs," confessed another.

Me? My first time was slow and sweet, passionate

and perfect — until my mother walked in on us. Wish I were kidding.

It's true that "today's teens" are dealing with brand new issues. Puberty happens earlier than it used to. Music videos dare 11-year-olds to wear booty shorts and shake body parts whose very functions they have yet to comprehend. And explicit digital photos — which we all know seem like a ducky idea at the time — can circulate through campus infinitely faster than a dog-eared Polaroid ever could.

But I wonder if girls today are actually smarter about sex than I ever was. More knowledgeable. More conscientious. That's what it seemed like recently, when I sat in on a Sexual Wisdom workshop for teenage girls.

Run by therapist Jennifer Freed, the 10-week group aims to help teens make informed decisions about sex by fostering casual, confidential conversations about everything from flirtation to masturbation, virginity to pornography. On a recent Monday night, a dozen Santa Barbara girls aged 14 to 18 trickled into Freed's living room-like therapy office. Some are there at the suggestion of school counselors, or their parents. Some come simply out of curiosity.

Dressed in sweatshirts and jeans, they plop onto couches and armchairs, dip into a bag of organic snacks, and start talking about sex.

A girl announces that her boyfriend wants them both to date other people. Freed asks the group to rate, on a scale of one to 10, one being lowest, how comfortable they'd be with such an "open relationship." When no one goes above four, she explained that women's hormones make us want to bond, and that sharing partners may actually be harder for women than men.

"I'm kind of on a crusade," said Freed, who cofounded the Academy of Healing Arts for area teens. "One third of girls will have had sexual intercourse by the time they're 14 — so they'd better know what that means for them."

Abstinence education is a joke, she said. "That doesn't help anybody in the midst of teen lust." So instead of advising them to resist "sexting" (sending nude phone-to-phone photos of themselves), for instance, Freed asks them, "'What motivates us to do that? Why is it exciting and interesting? And what are the consequences of this?' You have to slow it all down so they can really examine the emotional aspects of the choices."

The workshop operates on donations and includes Freed's workbook, which prompts participants to write or draw responses to questions like, "How would you react if someone walked in on you during sex?"

And believe me when I say that's one you want to think about before it happens.

Sexile

CAN COLLEGES BAN DORM SEX?

IT WASN'T EVEN SUNRISE when I felt nature's call. Clad in my usual sleepwear — yesterday's T-shirt, unfussy undies — I stumbled half-dreaming from my twin bed toward the loo and stopped cold as I shuffled past my roommate's bed in the opposite corner of the narrow room.

Was that a hairy arm hanging out of the bed? Was that a man's sleeping body entwined with that of my sacked-out roommate, only inches from my barely garbed, bathroom-bound bladder?

He hadn't been there when I went to sleep. What had happened in here? Scratch that. I didn't want to know. Could I possibly go back to sleep mere feet from this rather attractive stranger? And if I left the room in my skivvies, how long before they'd clear out and I could return?

Tufts University drew nationwide shrugs and sniggers last month when it issued an edict to students: "You may not engage in sexual activity while your roommate is present in the room."

It's funny. It is. But finding somewhere to bump bodies in college really is an exacting task. I remember breaking into empty dorm rooms and, once, climbing onto a campus rooftop. Not safe. Not smart. Not especially sanitary.

"I had an apartment sophomore year with a small dining room that we dubbed 'The Love Room,'" says a guy I went to school with. In theory, the space was available to any of the four roommates, but one guy hit a lucky streak and began hogging it nightly. "Total 'Love Room' monopoly. We eventually had to create a schedule."

As long as there have been co-ed colleges, students have found discreet ways to warn roommates when their room is, well, occupied: a neck-tie/tube sock/poofy hair-band on the doorknob or, say, a brief but impassioned text message.

But what of those who aren't so thoughtful? Who follow their jolly wherever it leads them, regardless of who's in the room?

"Waking up to the sound of soft moans," says a current UCSB student, "and seeing a lump in my roommate's bed moving in a caterpillar motion never puts an optimistic spin on the rest of the day."

"At UCSB, many of my friends debate the pros and cons of bunk beds," adds another. You can't actually see what's happening on your roomie's mattress, "but you can certainly feel the bed shaking, which might be more horrifying."

Some students wonder how you enforce a rule like Tufts'. "If roommates are disrespectful enough to do that while you're in the room," adds a City College alum, "then what makes you think they're respectful enough to follow the rule?"

Besides, "rules" and "sex" make strange bedfellows.

"Sex will happen where there are horny, beautiful people," says a current UC Berkeley student, "and this just so happens to be the case on college campuses."

True dat. You just can't mash a bunch of hard-bodied single people into a room and force them to read pulse-quickening Othello or study the principles of magnetism and expect them to be chaste. To behave. To refrain from ripping off each other's backpacks and diving for each other's midterms.

Since we know it's gonna happen — even stuffy old Tufts acknowledges it now — campuses should provide little rooms where students can enjoy a private coupling. Like restrooms, they'd be just another place where humans can carry out their base but natural urges. Call them Fornication Stations, perhaps, and provide free contraception in an attractive basket.

Until then, students will have to suffer through the imperfect, and often invasive, sexual culture that pervades campuses. On the bright side, you sometimes meet interesting people as you're tip-toeing past your roommate's crowded bed.

Remember the hairy-armed guy? I married him.

On Decent Proposals

IT'S JUNE. WEDDING SEASON. Only a few days left to dig out that embossed invitation, navigate your buddy's online bridal registry, and take a Sharpie to the scuffs on your party shoes.

During the reception, the deejay will spin "Single Ladies," and you'll want to hit the dance floor and show off your mad self-spanking skills. But the groom's gabby Aunt Joan and sozzled Uncle Ted will stop you to tell The Story. The treasured "How He (or She) Proposed" anecdote. It's told and retold at these events, laying the foundation for the couple's mutual mythology, the oral history of their romance.

Our culture loves a good "Will you marry me?" narrative. It's the dragon-slaying folktale of our modern world. How'd he do it? How'd he fell the beast? Did he use wit, or brawn? Did he bury the ring in bean dip or convince the philharmonic to bust out Dramarama's "Anything, Anything," falling to one knee and wailing,

"Marry me, marry me, marry me …"?

Outrageous proposals abound in recent news. A San Diego tattoo artist inked "Rachel, will you marry me?" onto his own leg. (I'd marry him for his perfect punctuation, but that's my freak-ness weakness.) A New Jersey valedictorian popped the question by calling her beau and fellow grad to the stage after her speech. A New York fella edited himself into *Back to the Future,* rented a movie theater, and took his girlfriend to see the flick — in which he shows up on screen, looks into the camera, and asks her to be his wife. They all said yes. Aww.

But over-the-top marriage proposals make me uneasy. First, they pressure the askee to say "I do." You have to sort of hate a guy to turn him down after he asks for your hand on the big screen at Staples Center during the Lakers playoffs. They also create an absurd standard of one-upmanship that has no place in real romance: "No, no, skywriting's been done! I need dolphins, damn it, dolphins that sing!"

Don't get me wrong; I applaud creativity. I know a guy who took his true love to dinner, disappeared into the men's room, and re-emerged in a velvet Prince Charming costume with tights and beret. They lived happily ever after.

There's even a dude on YouTube who orchestrated the mind-boggling coup of having a skyscraper's windows light up to spell out "Lisa will you marry me?" while they stood out front at night. (Note the missing comma; I'm just saying.)

But here's my biggest beef with Grandiose Proposals: Are they indicative of the kind of marriage that will follow?

After the cake has been ordered, the garter tossed, and the gifts exchanged for cash to pay for all the crap they bought on their honeymoon, these newlyweds have to live together. Like forever. Will their union be as inspired as the proposal that sparked it?

I heard about a guy who wrote "Will you marry me?" on a tortilla chip (See? A Sharpie's uses are myriad) and had a waiter hide it in the chip basket at his gal's favorite taqueria. The stunt showed foresight, imagination, whimsy — but will those qualities make him an ideal spouse? Will she ever again feel so special, so all-important, so worth his trouble? Hard to say. But I did enjoy typing all those commas.

The best proposal story I ever heard goes like this: A guy gets up in the middle of the night to use the can, comes back to bed and mutters, apropos of nothing, "That reminds me ... will you marry me?"

Extravagant? Romantic? Promising? No. But I'd have given anything to hear Aunt Joan recount that pretty parable as the cake was cut.

Should Marriage Expire?

COUPLEHOOD IS LAID OUT in chapters. One chapter is rife with romance as your peers get hitched. The next is replete with pride as your peers have babies.

The next — the one I'm in now — is saturated with shock, anxiety, and discouragement as your peers bicker, cheat, and surrender their once-happy marriages to the life-hacking bandsaw that is divorce.

It's ugly. Though my marriage feels sturdy, it's hard not to wince and take cover, whimpering, under the storm of blame lobbing, heart wringing, and estate dividing that so many friends are weathering.

With national divorce rates around 50 percent, are half of us doomed to betray or grow apart from the partners we promised to have and hold? Are we damned to disillusionment for failing to cherish 'til death do us part?

Our grandparents managed to stay married, either through a stronger commitment to wedlock or a greater tolerance for misery. But if splits are inevitable in today's live-for-the-moment culture, then can't they be — shouldn't they be — less painful?

What if, when our spouses' faults begin outshining their favors and that irresistible yen for newness comes a-knockin', we could gracefully excuse ourselves from the union with no hard feelings? What if marriage were a temporary construct? What if it simply expired, like milk?

Last year, the Australian Bureau of Statistics floated the idea of fixed-term marriage contracts: A marriage license would expire after five years, and 10 years, unless the couple renewed it. They hoped such a construct would encourage partners to work proactively toward surpassing those milestones, and remove the stigma associated with divorce so that it wouldn't feel like a failure, but the natural course of many relationships.

If we had to "re-up" every five years, perhaps we wedded folk would be on our best behavior: attentive, communicative, engaged, and more apt to slip into seductive satin than saggy sweatpants at the end of the day. Then again, maybe a looming renewal date would create anxiety, rendering null one of the best parts of marriage: the not-having-to-always-be-fabulous-because-they-love-you-anyway perk.

"I think if you're going into a marriage with an 'out clause,' then you probably shouldn't be getting married in the first place," said a friend of mine.

But if we stopped imagining marriage as an everlasting fairy tale, if we instead approached it as a series of satisfying, self-contained chapters, we might be more successful.

"It works for jogging," another friend concurred. "I can't quite commit to jogging a whopping five miles, but I can commit to going to that next tree, and then the next fence, and then that mailbox. Pretty soon, I realize I went the whole five miles."

A divorced friend of mine doesn't like the idea. "I am not available for lease," she said. "I don't want to be driven around for a few years and then traded in for a newer model just because hey, it's in the contract."

It would be especially sticky if children were involved, but let's be honest: Couples divorce despite the proven benefits of a two-parent household. If they could walk away with a handshake and a "thanks, that was fun," it would be less taxing on the kids than an unplanned, unbridled war.

The greatest drawback to marital expiration dates, I think, is that couples who didn't expect to stay together wouldn't make long-term plans together. They wouldn't build. They wouldn't dream. They wouldn't hope.

And shared hope is really the brass ring of coupledom. In fact, if fixed-term marriages can't eradicate the perpetual threat of divorce, then mutual, matrimonial hope may be the best we can do. Eager to see what life's next chapter brings, I'm still hoping for a happy ending.

Bucking Monogamy

THOROUGHLY PERFORATED BY Puritanism, we Americans are quite sure that if something feels really, really good, it's probably very, very bad for you. Like shooting smack, watching porn on your boss's computer, or digging to the bottom of an order of Outback's Aussie Cheese Fries.

Love affairs are another example. In order to reap the toe-curling rewards of conventional romance — from the shivery intensity of new sex to the unparalleled peace of enduring intimacy — we must also abide the inevitable tedium of monogamy. We must accept and embrace the thrill-sapping sameness that yangs true love's yin.

Or must we?

A covey of free-thinking, free-loving dissidents is bucking Puritanism, bucking monogamy, and, frankly, bucking anyone else who's game. They practice what they call "polyamory," or being openly — and therefore ethically — involved in multiple intimate relationships.

"Poly," as it's called for short, encompasses all sorts of consciousness-expanding configurations: from stick-straight to gay-as-the-day-is-long, from married couples with separate-but-not-secret lovers to a trio of adoring roommates who share more than the water bill. It's not polygamy and it's not "swinging." It's consensual non-monogamy with as much emphasis on love as on sex.

"People tend to harp on the sexual component, but the relationship component is just as important," said Thomas Amoroso in the *Boston Globe*'s recent story about the phenomenon. Amoroso is a Massachusetts ER doctor and poly practitioner who shares a female life partner with another man.

Today's polyamorists aren't the first to reject the traditional one-on-one courtship and marriage model; surely, intriguing romantic arrangements have been made behind closed doors for centuries.

But spurred, perhaps, by recent nationwide debate about the definition of marriage, and united into regional groups via the Internet (there isn't currently an active group in Santa Barbara), their numbers appear to be growing. Coined in the 1990s by a self-described "neo-pagan poet," the word "polyamory" is in both the Merriam-Webster and Oxford English dictionaries. Experts estimate more than half a million people in the U.S. engage in openly polyamorous relationships.

For old-skool copulators like myself, the concept can be unsettling. I think about polyamory and my "naughty" alarms go off, especially when I hear about the poly guy who told *Portland Monthly* magazine that his missus serves him and his girlfriends post-coital snacks. "There's nothing sexier than having your wife bring you food when you're in bed with another woman," he said with no apparent shame.

How can this be right? Why is he allowed to have intimacy, trust, and variety, damn him? But when I shake off any socially conditioned priggishness, it's hard to find real fault. It's not heartless if you're connecting with someone emotionally; it's not dishonest if everyone consents.

Logically, then, the only fair question is whether you can truly be in love with more than one person at a time: Does adding a second lover necessarily subtract from your bond with the first? I've heard that hurt feelings can still occur between poly playmates; just because there's no betrayal doesn't mean there's no jealousy.

I know a married mom from Santa Barbara who's polyamorous — but her beloved husband isn't. And he's not crazy about her two long-term lovers. "I don't necessarily believe in the limits that we place on relationships in a traditional marriage," she said. "I believe that the more people you love, the better your life will be. I believe in flexibility in thinking."

Indeed, it takes an open mind to properly ponder poly's ethical and emotional geometry. Assume, for starters, that its devotees look just like the rest of us prudes. They're not witchy weirdos with lust in their eyes; they're artists and engineers, realtors and baristas.

And the much-loved mom above? No kidding: She's a wedding planner.

Once Upon
Two Mattresses

STANDING NAKED AT the bedside, my man and I tear back the covers, anticipating ecstasy. We climb between the sheets and press together, limbs entwined. Our eyes close in mutual euphoria and we fall … rapturously … asleep. (That's right, pervs. Asleep.)

It's our cherished nightly ritual: tug comforter up to noses, whisper, "Don't tell them where we are," and huddle pod-like 'til morning. Our shared shuteye is a horizontal dance — not a provocative bop but a slumber rhumba. Throughout the night, we flop subconsciously apart and back together, finding ourselves reconnected by morning's first light: feet stacked, knees overlapping, fingertips resting on shoulders.

So for us, the following news was a rude awakening: Almost a quarter of American couples sleep in separate beds or bedrooms, according to the National Sleep Foundation. And builders claim the demand for separate master suites is on the rise.

I thought his-and-hers bunks were a relic from the *I Love Lucy* days — and even then, a fake-out to placate easily titillated network execs. Who wants to trot off to dreamland solo when you've got a buddy to spoon?

There's a traditional Armenian wedding toast: "May you grow old on one pillow." Surely intimacy must suffer when couples sleep in separate beds. I mean, you could schedule erotic mid-house meet-ups, but, frankly, most of us just aren't that proactive: If we're rarely prone and alone, it might never happen.

What of pillow talk, too? Bedtime is when couples share those inane bits o' babble ("So I ran into what's-his-name today at Pascucci …") that keep us connected, attuned to one another's emotional gauges. Could we stay close without a nightly exchange of useless minutiae?

It turns out lots of couples I know (and chances are you know them, too; it's a small town) hit the sack in entirely different rooms. And for lots of great reasons. Log-sawing is chief among them.

"You're a lot more likely to have good a.m. sex," argues one friend, "with someone who didn't just piss you off by keeping you up all night snoring the roof off the house."

Some couples have opposing sleep habits: "He likes a ton of quilts; I like one sheet," says a mom who has her own bedroom. "He gets up at 4 a.m. to exercise; I stay up late. Both of us are light sleepers and both of us snore. Why should we follow convention when it means both of us would be sleep-deprived?"

Another hip couple sleeps on two distinct twin mattresses on a king-sized frame; it looks "normal" to houseguests, "but under that façade, we have completely different sheets and covers," she confesses, "which solves the following annoyances: You don't get kicked, you don't sweat under excessive piles of wool blankets, and you're entirely covered by your sheets in the morning."

Hey, couplehood is complex, so I'll give kudos to anyone who can make it work, even if it means dual nightlights.

I know a guy who sleeps in a different bed than his wife. In another bedroom. On the opposite side of the house.

"It's the best of both worlds," he says. "You can still 'visit' each other, but have the freedom to keep your own sleep schedules and patterns.

"The real relationship saver, though? Separate bathrooms."

Stud or Schlub

LUST ON THE RED CARPET

T HERE ARE CERTAIN THINGS a woman is supposed to have accumulated by this point in her life. A signature perfume. A conversation-stopping potluck recipe. And a Hollywood hunk of choice.

I have none of these things, and I spend little time fretting over it. But I must admit that each year at Academy Awards time, I grapple with some shame that I have no favorite man candy to ogle on the red carpet.

I tend to watch the awards shows surrounded by opinionated gal pals and, for the most part, I can holler tasteless comments with the best of them. We gasp and grouse over actresses' necklines, waistlines, and panty lines. My specialty is the bitchy accessory crack: e.g., "What is that in her hair, a Krispy Kreme?" or "Earrings or necklace, honey, not both."

It's when my friends start hooting and gyrating over the bow-tied, limo-emerging actors — bedroom-eyed Clooney, swollen-lipped Pitt, square-jawed Brosnan —

that I find myself bored and heading to the kitchen for more artichoke dip.

I can't help it. I'm just not attracted to most leading men. With the exception of Harrison Ford (who crushed my crush when he left the wife for the waif), broad-shouldered, steely-gazed, Armani-clad blockbuster stars have never done it for me. Not pretty-boy Leonardos or cool-as-ice Denzels. Not cocksure bad boy Colin Farrell or edgy artiste Johnny Depp. And I've never been Baldwin-prone.

My own mother recently was shocked to discover that I don't get weak-kneed for Daniel Craig or dizzy for Russell Crowe. I wasn't sure if she was affronted, like I was insulting her boyfriends, or if she was genuinely worried, like I might be missing some vital chromosome.

"Okay," she prodded, "then who is your favorite movie guy? Who do you like to watch?"

"Well," I stalled, "I like that guy … the one in that movie … I mean, there are tons!"

But the truth is, there aren't. There are only a handful of actors who tickle my hormones, and none of them (sadly, for me) has ever played a sweaty gladiator, tormented vigilante, or alien-battling soldier. It's hard to even picture any of them punching a photographer or dating a stripper in their real lives.

Because none of them are studs. In fact, they're more schlubs. But they're smart, funny, and understated, and that's my weird little recipe for Hollywood hot. You won't hear me shout, "Hey, baby, who are you wearing? Can it be me?" when these fellas shuffle down the red carpet.

Because if they're even invited to the Oscars, they get camera-blocked by the Tom Cruises and Will Smiths — the usual statuette-hogging beefcakes.

So I've come up with a special set of awards for the guys whose faces rarely make magazine covers, but whose anti-star quality gets my popcorn popping:

Best Schlub Who Looks Hunky by Comparison to Everyone Else in the Judd Apatow Movies:
Paul Rudd

Best Schlub I've Had a Crush on Since Puberty:
Jason Bateman

Best Schlub Who's Even Sexy When He Frenches Heath Ledger:
Jake Gyllenhaal

Best Schlub Whom I Have a Hard Time Admitting I'm Attracted To:
Steve Carell

Best Schlub with a Severely Crooked Nose, and the Lone Blond Schlub of the Bunch:
Owen Wilson

Schlub by Which All Other Schlubs Will Forever Be Judged, and Lose:
John Cusack

Going to Bed Angry

I DID IT. I WENT to bed angry. They tell you not to, but I did. And I lived to tell the tale.

We were in bed, having one of those "Why can't you just say the right thing?"/"Why can't you just tell me what to say?" arguments, when my eyes began stinging from lack of sleep. So I shut them. Just for a second, just to rest. But I maintained a fabulously formidable scowl to show my opponent that our spat was still very much in play.

I woke up seven hours later — scowling — and even more outraged than I'd been the night before. The row was unresolved and now we had broken the cardinal rule of couplehood, too; no good could come of this ...

It was only weeks ago, while lunching at Stella Mare's, that we got to chatting with an elderly couple sitting near us. Holding hands and beaming like the stars of a Cialis commercial, they told us their "secret": "Never go to bed angry."

Seriously? I thought. That's it? That lame old saw? I'd never really understood the adage because I never go to bed angry. I can't. To me, going to bed mad means I've lost the argument. Which is something I don't do willingly.

"I have a tough time sleeping until I have my say!" echoes a friend who has woken her husband at 2 a.m. just to make a painstakingly worded point.

Some friends agree that disputes should end when the day does. "There's nothing worse," says a young woman I know, "than waking up the next morning only to realize, 'Great, we still have that to deal with.'"

But should such disagreements be debated on your pillow-top Posturepedic? "Go to bed mad, but don't go to sleep mad," advises one husband. "Work out the kinks while you're warm and cozy. Beds don't have doors to slam — and turning over and looking away is not nearly as frustrating as walking away."

Others say bed is the first place they head when they're pissed at their partners. "I'm too tired to deal with it at night, which isn't conducive to a rational discussion," says one gal.

If you're lucky, sleep can do more than mitigate a fight; it can prevent it outright. "I've gone to bed angry and woken up happy that I didn't express it the night before," admits another friend. "Morning light seems to shrink the issues."

So, is the best marital advice really, "Pay no attention to what old people tell you about relationships"? Is the old "sleep secret" just so much hooey?

"I give it a fair amount of truth," says S.B. therapist Gary Linker, PhD. "I don't think that prolonged anger helps a relationship. That doesn't mean that if we're angry, we need to decide at 11 or 12 o'clock at night that we need to thoroughly resolve this issue right now."

He suggests that couples listen to — and in fact hear — each other's viewpoints, then agree to revisit the issue tomorrow. "When there's at least a plan in place, then that anger dissipates and the goodwill, the foundational base of the relationship, is reestablished."

Or you can endure the kind of odious morning-after that I did: stomping around the house muttering infantile slurs and finally confronting the culprit, who — I swear to you — had no memory of the tiff whatsoever. Which taught me that couplehood is too capricious to rely on trite rules of thumb. You've got to be flexible and open-minded.

So the next time I'm livid at lights-out, I'm going to try this new tack from a sensible gal I know: "I say go to bed mad. And plan your revenge."

The Love Contract

EVERYONE KNOWS YOU'RE not supposed to date your boss. It makes things messy at the office.

I dated mine once, and can attest that things did get messy at the office. Also in the car. And on the sofa at his place.

We flirted. We kissed. We got naked. Shacked up, got married, had kids. Even now, we continue to grope each other in front of the subordinates, open each other's mail, and answer our home phone singing, "Aloha! Deano's Weiner Shanty" — all behavior that is really frowned upon in a corporate setting.

Mr. Boss Man and I were in college when we began canoodling among the cubicles, and our tryst failed to raise a ruckus. Some colleagues offered high-fives; others rolled their eyes and made occasional gagging sounds. Most just dismissed us as indiscreet young idiots.

Today, though, employees who date coworkers may be asked to sign a "love contract" declaring their romantic

BED, WRATH & BEYOND

alliance. Known formally as "consensual relationship agreements," these documents confirm that both parties willingly entered into the affair, and that either one is free to end it without professional ramifications.

I saw one that read, "The undersigned independently and collectively desire to undertake and pursue a mutually consensual social and/or amorous relationship ..."

Whew! Makes me hot just reading it.

Supposedly inspired by former president Bill Clinton's disastrous dalliances with a certain White House intern, the contracts aim to protect companies from sexual harassment lawsuits in the event of an ugly breakup. Which sounds to me like corporate code for "we need a foolproof way for top execs to continue playing with the hearts and pencil-skirted posteriors of our delicious, er, ambitious new hires. Have Legal get on this ..."

"Love contracts" haven't yet been tested in court, but they've been mocked plenty in prime time. The amorous casts of both *The Office* and *Grey's Anatomy* have endured the humiliating and admittedly hilarious process of having to reduce the precious first buds of passion to a page of tedious legal jargon on file with HR.

You can see why bureaucrats would champion such a contract. More than 40 percent of workers confess to having dated a fellow employee, and experts say high divorce rates, later marriages, and a record number of working women will likely lead to more and more office flings. It's hard to be productive when your lover's dreamy voice is citing sales statistics just down the hall, and it's tricky being diplomatic when your pookie bear is one of several associates up for a promotion. Love and lust are workplace distractions, but no-dating policies are notoriously difficult to enforce.

Are "love contracts" really the answer? If corporations could truly make rationally behaving robots out of all their employees simply by having them sign conduct agreements, they really ought to start with a "Don't Snap at the Receptionist Just Because You're Hungry" contract or a "Won't Get Plastered at Lunch No Matter How Awful That Meeting Was" pledge.

Humans — even those in power suits — are ruled by emotions. And emotions are spastically, sprawlingly, spectacularly messy. Emotions shouldn't be defined in corporate terms, and they can't be reduced to a legal document with any significance.

But perhaps intra-office affairs aren't as big a threat as companies fear.

Last month, Costco asked members in various states if they thought workers should sign "love contracts." Melvin Williams of Duncanville, Texas, said no, arguing that it's the employees' responsibility to keep their relationships out of the office.

His personal code? "Never get your honey where you make your money."

Take This Ring and...

ARRIAGES BEGIN WITH the promising plink of ritual: aisle-marching, veil-lifting, rice-flinging. But they end with the unceremonious thud of reality: stacks of documents, pained court appearances, crammed moving vans.

In Japan, a nation where ritual is revered and divorce is on the rise, couples have found a way to bring the same pomp, poignance, and purpose to their breakup as they did to their nuptials: divorce ceremonies.

Since last year, entrepreneur Hiroki Terai has officiated more than 20 such ceremonies at his Tokyo "divorce mansion." He charges to help divorcing couples mark the end of their relationship and take a vow to begin their lives anew. Ex-husband- and ex-wife-to-be ride to the event in separate rickshaws and smash their wedding rings with a gavel as friends cheer. Divorcés say they feel relief — even release — when it's over.

More typically in the States, folks have separate

celebrations when their divorces are finalized: "I'm going to have one this month when the cord cuts," says a spouse-sloughing friend of mine. "But it's going to be with girlfriends at a bar. I thought I would burn the wedding license and auction his wedding band — you know, the one he took off when he dated other women."

I asked several Santa Barbara wedding officiants if they had ever performed a divorce ceremony; none had. Most had never heard of such a thing. And at least one bristled at the notion.

"A divorce celebration? Boy, that's a strange contradiction in terms," says Scot Saunders of Montecito Weddings. "As a minister, that's just a hard one to swallow."

But if divorces are going to take place — and according to statistics, they are — then why shouldn't we find a way to make them more bearable? What if such ceremonies could be respectful? What if they could bring peace?

The Unitarian Church has a divorce ritual called a "ceremony of hope" in which both husband and wife ask for forgiveness and release each other from their promises of betrothal. Kind of nice, right? Kind of mature and cool.

Beverly Plummer is an interfaith minister who wrote a divorce ceremony a few years ago. "Closure is very important, especially when children are involved," says Plummer, who suggests inviting the kids to be a part of the proceedings. "My ceremony has phrases that say, 'We are not together, but we love you and we will always be your parents.'"

She hasn't yet had occasion to perform it — and wonders if she ever will. Let's face it; divorce is draining. And organizing an un-wedding takes effort that many splitting couples simply don't have to spare. "Once you get through what you have to get through," conceded Plummer, "you're out of energy around that other person."

In fact, the contentious nature of divorce may prevent the Amicable Un-Wedding trend from ever really taking off. If you can no longer even sit across the dinner table from your one-time love, how are you two ever going to agree on a divorce ceremony guest list? And then there's the cake ...

"I've been contending for years that we should have an official, spiritual ceremony for divorce. It is, after all, a major milestone in any life," says nuptial officiant Marlene Morris, of A Central Coast Wedding. "But the truth is often that feelings are still too raw, too many hurtful words have been spoken, or the individuals involved are still too angry or feel too betrayed."

Perhaps she's right. I asked a friend of mine, who endured a combative divorce, whether she would have considered participating in a cordial divorce ceremony in front of their friends. "Yeah, that wouldn't have worked," she retorted instinctively. "He didn't have any friends."

The Art of the Come-On

THE PERFECT COME-ON. It's the Holy Grail of dating, the enchanted key that unlocks the glorious gates of Eternal, On-Demand Lady Lovin'. Many seek it. Many fail.

"Shoot, I seem to have lost my phone number. Can I have yours?"

"If I could rearrange the alphabet, I'd put U and I together."

"Did you clean your pants with Windex? Because I can practically see myself in them."

The notion that a single pick-up line could win a woman's heart, or even convince her to doff her Hanky Pankies for an exceedingly pleasant 37 minutes, is so far-fetched I'd swear it were a myth. Except that, occasionally, it works.

I was sitting outside a Denny's recently, waiting for my family to arrive. A couple of young guys were walking in when one stopped and said, "Excuse me?"

I turned, expecting him to say that I'd dropped my car keys. Or forgotten to put on pants. You know, the usual.

"I just want to tell you, I think you're really pretty," he said.

And that was it. No creepy alligator smile. No goofy drunk-on-the-dance-floor body language. Just "you're really pretty," a shy grin, and he moseyed into the eatery.

I'll be honest. If I had been single, I would have followed that fella inside, slid into his oversized booth, and ordered up his Moons Over My Hammy, if you know what I mean. (No, I don't, either, but I would have figured it out, I assure you.)

As it is, his comment made my day, which is a little bit embarrassing. And a little bit confusing. How is it that a wolf whistle can make a gal feel cheap, vulnerable, and somehow guilty ("I *knew* I shouldn't have worn this dress downtown"), but an artless compliment can leave her girlishly giddy?

I feel for guys, I do. It's not easy trying to charm a woman. You work up the courage to make a move, heed your instincts, seize the moment, and — like the tollbooth worker who called my friend "babe" and touched her palm as he gave her change — all you get is an "eww! yucky!" in return. And what works with one gal may not work with another. Some swoon for one-liners like, "Did the sun come out or did you just smile at me?" whereas such a string of words might cause me to vomit violently.

I do have a weakness for funny. My friend Chris says his best line is, "Can I buy you six drinks?" Who wouldn't let him buy her at least the one?

My girlfriends say the best come-ons are respectful, authentic, and precisely tailored to the recipient. Also, this works well: "Hi."

But here's a little secret. The real reason my pancake-pursuing suitor (let's call him Denny) made me beam rather than cringe is that he walked away. Perhaps he got a closer look and realized I was old enough to be his, um, aunt. His obscenely cool and unreasonably gorgeous aunt. Or perhaps he spotted the glob of lime-green Play-Doh in my hair. Whatever.

What mattered, from my perspective, was that his flattery had no purpose other than to make me feel good. And that's the key to the charming come-on, guys. It must be uttered not with the intent of scoring, but with the sole purpose of making her happy. The great irony, of course, is that if you genuinely mean it — if her feelings are your first priority — then you're worthy of her and you'll hit a home run.

Or a Grand Slam, if you're at Denny's.

INDEX

ABOUT THE AUTHOR

STARSHINE ROSHELL is an award-winning journalist, nationally syndicated columnist and the author of *Keep Your Skirt On: Kicky Columns With Legs*. Her work has appeared in *The Hollywood Reporter, New York Post, Ventura Star, Roanoke Times, Santa Barbara Independent,* and *Westways, Miller-McCune, Hybrid Mom* and *Houston Family* magazines. She lives in utopia.

Breinigsville, PA USA
20 October 2010
247748BV00002B/1/P